SCi

How do business founders not only start a business but ensure sustainable growth for the future? This book provides the tools and understanding that enable successful business growth at the scale-up stage.

Scale-up and Build Your Business distils the author's two decades of working with high-growth, high-performing independently owned and managed businesses, including Cobra Beer, Hotel Chocolat, Belvoir Cordials, Thatcher's Cider, Pacific Direct and Go Ape. Over many years David Molian and his colleagues have identified both the drivers that accelerate growth and the blockers that prevent it. Through case histories, industry analyses and numerous examples this book details five key challenges faced by ambitious entrepreneurs, and documents how they overcome them. For each key challenge, this book describes the accelerators and bear traps which will help or hinder the journey to successful growth and the creation of long-term, sustainable, independent value that translates into successful exit.

The lessons within this book will be invaluable for policy-makers, advisors and ambitious business founders who want to turn a start-up into a successful and sustainable company. In a period marked by uncertainty and economic stagnation, this guide is more vital than ever.

David Molian was for many years Director of Cranfield's Business Growth Programme, the UK's longest-running scale-up programme for company founders. He has served as faculty at business schools in the UK and France and advised national government policy-makers.

SCALE-UP AND BUILD YOUR BUSINESS

HOW TO RECOGNISE AND OVERCOME THE CRITICAL CHALLENGES OF BUSINESS GROWTH AND EXIT

David Molian

Routledge
Taylor & Francis Group

LONDON AND NEW YORK

Designed cover image: Getty Images / erhui1979

First published 2024
by Routledge
4 Park Square, Milton Park, Abingdon, Oxon OX14 4RN

and by Routledge
605 Third Avenue, New York, NY 10158

Routledge is an imprint of the Taylor & Francis Group, an informa business

British Library Cataloguing-in-Publication Data
A catalogue record for this book is available from the British Library

ISBN: 978-1-032-53156-4 (hbk)
ISBN: 978-1-032-53157-1 (pbk)
ISBN: 978-1-003-41061-4 (ebk)

DOI: 10.4324/9781003410614

Typeset in Bembo
by Newgen Publishing UK

CONTENTS

Foreword   vi

Acknowledgments   ix

Introduction: growth, and why it matters   1

1   Challenge to growth number one: stick to the knitting   24

2   Challenge to growth number two: money, money, money   46

3   Challenge to growth number three: managerial styles   72

4   Challenge to growth number four: sustainable points of difference   98

5   Challenge to growth number five: reinventing the business to build further value   119

Afterword   155

FOREWORD

Whether it's a country or a company, growth is key to survival and success. David Molian's book hits the nail on the head in explaining and analysing in detail the importance of growth and creating value through growth.

I have had the privilege of working closely with David for many years, ever since I attended the Business Growth Programme at the Cranfield School of Management 25 years ago. The Business Growth Programme changed my life and my businesses, not only by engaging me in lifelong learning but in educating me in detail on how to grow a business. David has been engaged with this programme and has seen and taught firsthand the business leaders on this course, which has been running for 35 years.

The businesses and people on this course have actively wanted to grow their business in the UK, where there are five and a half million small and medium-sized businesses, accounting for 60% of all employment, over 50% of private sector turnover, and over 99% of all businesses by number. *Scale-up and Build Your Business* examines in detail the drivers of business growth, both external and internal, and the importance of cash, acknowledging the age-old saying, "turnover is vanity, profit is sanity, but cash flow is reality".

David Molian also details the barriers and challenges to growth; the accelerants, bear traps, and blockers, and what makes a business sustainable and what, by extension, enables sustainable business growth. The book also emphasises the importance of good corporate citizenship and is full of real-life case studies from participants in the Business Growth Programme, many of whose alumni are now some of Britain's most successful examples of entrepreneurship; Hotel Chocolat, Go Ape, let alone, may I humbly say, my own business, Cobra Beer, now a household name. The book is full of amazing insights, including showing how not all opportunities are equal, the dangers of taking your eye off the ball, the importance of knowing your customer, the virtue of keeping it simple, how to find new customers, the diversification trap, and finding and building a niche.

David also frankly explains many realities: for example, entrepreneurs frequently underestimate how long it takes to establish their market position, often diversifying too early; making money is simple, but it isn't easy! The book goes into great detail in outlining business models that work and all aspects of finance, including, but not limited to, profit, cash, margins, credit rating, and being creative in raising funding. It is an utterly comprehensive book, with every aspect of it resonating with me, for example the importance of control as well as the impact of a loss of control, fraud, which often emanates, sadly, from the enemy within, and the hard fact that profit and cash are not the same thing. Businesses go bust, not necessarily because they are not profitable but because they run out of money.

This book provides phenomenal insights into the managerial styles and approaches of entrepreneurs from the Artisan-Hero-Meddler-Strategist Model; how to be an effective leader; going from brand me to brand business; and the importance of creating a senior team. Moreover, it covers in depth the values of being different and better, being contrarian, creating a distinctive culture, and the need for constant reinvention, which means evolutionary business building and revolutionary business strategy. It covers business literally from end to end, including how to sell your business, how to transition from CEO to chairman, and how to value your company. I have not come across a better, more thorough, and all-rounded guide to growing a business and its entire ins and outs than David Molian's *Scale-up and Build Your Business*. It should be a must-read for every business school student, for every entrepreneur, and for every business leader.

Lord Karan Bilimoria, CBE DL
Founder and Chairman of Cobra Beer
Member of the House of Lords, UK Parliament

ACKNOWLEDGMENTS

Many hundreds, indeed thousands, of people have contributed to this book, although most are unlikely to be aware of doing so. The vast majority are those participants who have passed through the suite of start-up and growth programmes at Cranfield designed for ambitious business owners and their management teams. Without their willingness to talk freely about the challenges of growing their organisations, our understanding of how we, as teachers, mentors and researchers, can help them achieve their ambitions would be much diminished. In virtually every instance that journey towards creating a sustainable business with independent value is a rollercoaster ride. If starting a business is a daunting challenge, maintaining that momentum through years of relentless hard work, setbacks and disappointment is even tougher. When success comes, it is sweet and well-deserved. The constraints of space allow us in this book to tell the stories of only a fraction of those we have worked with over the years. There are many more unsung heroes, and they know who they are. We salute you, and all who have supported you along the way.I also owe a considerable debt of gratitude to my predecessors and successors as Directors of the Business Growth Programme, and the teams of counsellors without whom the delivery of this series of programmes would have been impossible. Many counsellors are themselves successful business owners who have passed through the programme and have elected to work on the Growth portfolio of programmes to nurture new generations of ambitious business founders and owners. Entrepreneurship is a team sport. The coaches may not be on the pitch, but their role is essential. The counsellors bring wisdom, experience and constructive challenge, as well as support and encouragement.Finally I would like to thank the many colleagues both at Cranfield University and institutions elsewhere, not just for their contributions to the Growth programmes but for all that we – collectively – have learned from them. We owe a particular thanks to Coutts & Co, which has provided bursaries for social entrepreneurs; to Evelyn Partners [formerly Smith & Williamson], who have been steadfast supporters of our programmes for many years; and to all those who have contributed to Cranfield's Evergreen Fund, which has given financial support to those who need a little extra help. And finally, thanks to my old comrade-in-arms, Paul Barrow, MBA FCA, from whose comments this book has greatly benefited.

Unless otherwise stated, all excerpts from case studies in this book are reproduced by permission of the copyright holder, Cranfield University.

INTRODUCTION: GROWTH, AND WHY IT MATTERS
CREATING VALUE THROUGH BUSINESS GROWTH

The primary *theme* of this book is the creation of sustainable value, by which I mean the scaling up of a business to create a valuable entity, independent of the business founder/owner. The primary *focus* of this book is on the stages of a business's development that follow once it has passed through the start-up and early formation phases, and shown that it is able not merely to survive but to thrive. The *lessons* for successful growth are drawn from the journeys of the several thousand ambitious business owners and founders who have passed through Cranfield School of Management in the last thirty-five years, principally through participation on the Business Growth Programme [BGP]. If I reproduced the entire content of the programme, this would be a very long book indeed. And as the programme has evolved continuously over three and a half decades such a task would be even harder. Instead, I have distilled what we collectively have learned from our own research, and what our participants have taught us, into

DOI: 10.4324/9781003410614-1

five key challenges, which are constant across time and business type. Recognising and overcoming these challenges is, I believe, critical to completing that journey as far as the founder/owner wishes to pursue it, and to creating the opportunity to crystallise that value: in simple terms, to turn wealth on paper into cash.

People start businesses for many different reasons. Research suggests that the main motivation is not, in fact, a desire to get rich, but the need for independence. Many of the entrepreneurs we have worked with over the years describe themselves as unemployable, or as unhappy employees in previous lives working for other people. Being their own boss suits their temperament and personality. In some instances, businesses are started not so much from choice but out of necessity, because of a lack of alternative employment opportunities. This is often the case with businesses set up by immigrants to a new country who lack the qualifications to enter many professions and thus have a highly restricted choice of employment. They have to create their own jobs, because others will not, and have a very strong incentive to succeed.[1]

Out of this population of business founders and owners, most are actually self-employed or freelancing. Huge numbers of skilled tradesmen and women build a business large enough to support themselves and their families. Perhaps over time they will take on one or two employees, or have loose associations with others in the same or complementary trades, but earning a living – and often quite a good one – is the limit of their ambitions. When the time comes to retire, these founders may hand over the reins to a younger family member, if that is what the next generation wants, but in virtually all cases the business itself has very little value in the market. Any value it *does* have is largely in the form of its list of customers and such reputation the owner has built up over a lifetime of trading. There is nothing particularly special which someone else cannot replicate: so why pay good money for it?

FOOD FOR THOUGHT #1

The vital six per cent, or why we need to take high-growth firms seriously

In the first decade of the 21st century, Nesta [The National Endowment for Science, Technology & the Arts] commissioned a study to establish the impact of high-growth small firms on the British economy. A high-growth firm is defined as having annual average growth *of at least 20 per cent* in employment or turnover over three years, with a minimum of ten employees in the initial year. Such firms are often described as gazelles.

Established firms (regardless of their size) created 3.4 million net jobs in 2002–05 and 2.9 million net jobs in 2005–08. **11,500 high-growth firms** accounted for 56 per cent of jobs created by existing businesses in 2002–05 and 43 per cent in 2005–08, or an average of 49.5 per cent between 2002 and 2008.

In comparison with their peer non-gazelles, high-growth firms generated between 3 and 3.5 times the number of new jobs in the respective time periods. When the two time periods are combined, the approximately 11,000 businesses which generated 20 per cent or more average annual employment growth over a three-year period were responsible for creating 54 per cent of new jobs.

In the follow-up survey that reviewed a time series of 2007–2010, using the same database, the authors observed exactly the same trend, namely that high-growth firms were responsible for generating half of the new jobs created by firms employing ten people or more. **Given that the British economy saw its worst recession for fifty years during this latter period, it seems reasonable to conclude that this phenomenon is**

resilient through the economic cycle. Moreover, the authors of these studies concluded that gazelles were to be found across all industry sectors and across different regions. In short, a mere fraction of the business population, the high performers, creates around half the nation's new employment.

Note: the analysis was drawn from the Business Structure Database compiled by the UK Office of National Statistics. The report, The Vital 6%, can be downloaded from the Nesta website.

The lack of any significant value in a self-employed enterprise compared with an "established" business is down to two things. First, in the self-employed business, whatever the legal form, the business and the owner/manager/founder are inextricable. You cannot in practice separate the one from the other. The founder is almost always the main income generator and salesperson and, without him or her, the business ceases to function. There are typically few assets in the firm as the net revenues are used to support the owner and their dependants. Second, there is limited potential – if any – to grow or "scale" the business. Such businesses tend to operate locally and invest very little in brand-building: their sales come from word of mouth, repeat orders from existing customers and some small-scale promotional activity. As a result of these two attributes, once the founder withdraws from the business it ceases to function as a going concern and customers will find others who can supply equivalent goods or services.

AMBITIOUS BUSINESS FOUNDERS

In mid-2022 there were around 5.5 million small businesses in the UK, that is to say enterprises employing between 0 and 49 people. In total, they accounted for three-fifths of all employment, or 16.3 mn individual workers. They represented 52 per cent of private sector turnover and over 99 per cent of the population of businesses. This structural pattern of small firm dominance is repeated across economies worldwide.

Within this population, in virtually every country, at any one time there exists a small group of business founders and owners who *actively want to grow* their businesses.[2] These enterprises are in direct contrast to the typical self-employed trader who is content with a certain level of sales and has no real desire to go beyond it. It is impossible to know exactly how large this population of ambitious business founders is, but we can say with confidence that it is a small proportion, and probably a fairly small proportion: the fact that government data shows most small businesses have either no employee or just one tells its own story. Within the south-east of England, which represents the main catchment area of participants on Cranfield's Business Growth Programme [BGP], we estimate there could be as many as 100,000 ambitious business founders. Yet even this upper limit is well under 10 per cent of the total small business population in the region.

WHAT DRIVES BUSINESS GROWTH?

Once the business founder with aspirations to grow is up and running, the possibilities of growth are determined by a mix of external and internal factors.

Externally, the most significant factors are the size of the opportunity, driven by customer demand, and the economic cycle. While a rising tide tends to lift all ships, a downturn is not necessarily bad news for everyone. Some businesses will continue to grow regardless of the economy, either because, like premium luxury goods, they are resilient despite the cycle or because they actually do better when most people have less money to spend [discount retailers, for instance].

Internally, the most important factors are the founder's appetite for growth, their energy and their capabilities as leader and manager. My experience suggests two other vital ingredients: the founder's **ability – or willingness – to change**, as the business grows and develops; and the **capacity of the business to scale**.

ARE YOU WILLING TO CHANGE – AND IS THE BUSINESS CAPABLE OF GROWTH?

The external factors are to a large extent outside the control of the founder. The internal factors most definitely are. Growth and, more particularly, **sustainable** growth happens very rarely by accident. It results from purposeful decisions, some small, some big, taken by the founder and the team which he or she has built around themselves. The *relevant* measures of growth are also liable to change over time. When asked to describe the scale of their business, a founder will most commonly cite the firm's turnover. Size, in the form of sales, really does seem to matter, at least to founders. But net profit and headcount may be no less important and actually more significant as measures of progress at different points in the firm's development. And then there is the generation of cash. Businesses do not go bust necessarily because they fail to make a profit. They unquestionably go bust when they run out of cash. As the old saying goes, turnover is vanity, profit is sanity but cashflow is reality.

TRANSITION TO GROWTH

The desire to grow a business is a necessary condition for growth, but it is not on its own enough. First, the business has to survive the launch into the market and early stages of life. That is no easy task. We know that most businesses will fail within a few years of start-up: some studies suggest within as little as three years. I have yet to meet a founder who didn't have challenges in the formative days, whether these are in the shape of acquiring customers, finding work-space, persuading suppliers to provide raw materials, goods or services, late payers, recruiting and retaining the right people – the list is endless. To overcome these, the founder needs the personal qualities of tenacity, self-belief, the power of persuasion, an indomitable worth ethic, robust health and the capacity to come back from rejection and setbacks. Luck also plays a part, but as the great South African golfer Gary Player put it, "the more I practise, the luckier I get".

As a general rule, once the business gets through those early days, the odds of continued survival progressively increase. For instance, the business that gets to year three has a fair chance of reaching year five, and if it gets to year five has an even better chance of getting to year ten. The founder has been tempered in the fire of those early stages and has emerged fitter [commercially, at least], stronger and more resilient as a consequence. At some point those firms which succeed will often increase their rate of growth, as measured by their expanding workforce, by three to three and a half times as much as their peers, earning themselves the title of *gazelles*. They are small in number, but pack a mighty economic punch.

THE IMPERATIVE TO CHANGE

In the course of this journey, the ambitious business encounters an inflection point, by which we mean an imperative to transition from survival mode to growth mode. In the early days, most of the founder's energies have been directed towards simply staying in business: to avoid running out of cash, for instance, or figuring out how to satisfy customers within the constraining resources of limited time, people and money. There are seldom enough hours in the day, people on deck or cash in the bank. However, many founders with aspirations to grow come to recognise that they are stuck in a loop of endlessly chasing their tail and, if the business is to grow, something – perhaps multiple things – has to change. To put it simply, you can't get to where you want to go by just doing what you've always done.

Some entrepreneurs attempt to make the change themselves and in a few cases, without any outside help or intervention, it works. All too often, however, it doesn't come off. Sales surge for a while, then fall back. Existing staff don't respond well to change and new recruits show early promise, but don't really fit in. The entry into what looks like a promising new market fails. Long-standing customers complain they aren't getting enough attention or, even worse, defect to the competition. Turnover goes up, but cash in the business shrinks. What is going on?

These and similar stories form a major part of the conversations that have taken place over nearly forty years with participants on the Cranfield Business Growth Programme. Occasionally I have even met business owners who have tried multiple times to grow their enterprises and never quite managed the trick.

There is no black art or mysterious process involved in growing a business successfully. In this book are laid out some well-established principles and guidelines which are derived from observing, researching and documenting how ambitious founders achieve their goals. I frame these as **barriers** or **challenges to growth** which founders need, first, to understand and second, to overcome. Again, I stress that these are intrinsic to the business and within the founder's/owner's control – providing he or she is prepared to change their management style, adapt their behaviour and spend their time differently. Each challenge merits a chapter all to itself, taking a deep dive into what the challenge consists of and strategies for dealing with it. In each chapter you will also find what we call the **accelerants** and **beartraps** or **blockers** that relate to each challenge.

ACCELERANTS, BEARTRAPS AND BLOCKERS

Accelerants are approaches which founders have used to take their businesses further and faster on the journey to growth. **Beartraps and blockers** are the common pitfalls that derail your plans and best endeavours: at the end of each chapter we identify the actions which will either speed up or hinder your business's journey to growth. We believe that you cannot underestimate the power of real-life examples, and so these accelerants, beartraps and blockers are illustrated by case studies of businesses that we have worked with and tracked over many years, often to the point of sale, when the entrepreneur crystallises the value they have created.

THE SUSTAINABLE BUSINESS *AND* SUSTAINABILITY

At this point, it is worth probing a little more deeply into what is meant by *sustainable*. As stated earlier, by a sustainable business I mean one which has enduring value that the founder/owner can at some point choose to turn into cash or "crystallise", as the venture capitalists call it. I say choose because along the journey there may be multiple opportunities to extract some of that value. Sometimes the opportunities are determined by the business owner[s], and sometimes by sheer chance or good fortune. The *test* of whether there is enduring value in a business is whether someone else is prepared to pay an acceptable price for some or all of it.

That said, "sustainable business" and by extension "sustainable business growth" have taken on a different sense in recent years, as sustainability itself has assumed a whole new meaning. I write these words as COP 27 is taking place in Sharm el Sheikh in Egypt, where thousands of politicians, business leaders and activists are gathering to debate the environmental agenda. At the top of the to-do list is the drive towards global decarbonisation and the acceleration of the green economy. For readers of this book, there are two important implications:

First, the momentum behind the green economy creates huge new opportunities for ambitious business founders. The transition to non-fossil fuel-dependent industries opens up the need for transformative technologies, processes, products and services. Best-positioned are those businesses which can straddle both sides of the transition. Take the case of CorrosionRADAR, a fast-growing business spun out of Cranfield University in 2017 and now based in Cambridge. The company's patented technology has created sensors that remotely monitor pipework corrosion under insulation in oil, gas and chemical refineries. This enables customers to detect, track and deal with rust and leaks early on, without the need for regular visual inspection on-site [and associated plant shutdowns]. The alternative, human inspection to check for such problems, is inherently hazardous, and the savings in time and money through adopting this technology are substantial. More to the point, the same approach can be used for the remote inspection and monitoring of wind farms and other forms of sustainable energy generation. CorrosionRADAR has a long future to look forward to.

Second, the pressures on business to behave as socially and environmentally responsible corporate citizens are growing more insistent. Some of that pressure takes the form of statutory requirements, which are themselves the result of public opinion and lobbying. For example, water companies in the UK are under increasingly stringent legal duties to clean up illegal discharges and ever higher fines for non-compliance because the British public are not prepared to tolerate polluted rivers and beaches strewn with sewage. This in turn drives scientific innovation to tackle these problems at source and thus creates new commercial opportunities. But much of this pressure for change arises internally, from inside business itself:

FOOD FOR THOUGHT #2

Good corporate citizenship: a growing imperative

From observations over the last decade of how a number of businesses have addressed the challenges of being good corporate citizens, lessons – or at the very least guidelines – can be inferred. For smaller, entrepreneurial or family-controlled businesses, the task is inherently easier, because the owners are not answerable to public markets and quarterly reporting demands. Their leaders have much greater freedom to set the tone and dictate the culture. Outdoor adventure specialist GoApe was founded by husband and wife team Tristram and Rebecca Mayhew, with sustainable development as a part of its DNA. In Britain their sites have been created in close association with the Forestry Commission and other landowners: today there are 35 locations in the UK, plus some 16 in the US. In 2022 the company was transferred into an Employee Ownership Trust, with the explicit aim of maintaining the ethos and values of the company in perpetuity.

Lesson number one: to embed such values in the core of a business, it's easier to start from scratch.

It's a rare business that has the luxury of beginning with a clean slate, but family businesses are also able to take the long view. Suffolk brewer Adnams is now entering its fifth generation of family stewardship. Its beers and spirits are distributed nationwide and the firm is by far the biggest employer in its home town of Southwold. For many years a highlight of the annual calendar has been the beach-cleaning, when the workforce turns out to scour and tidy the adjacent stretch of Suffolk coast. The company is also a long-time sponsor of local charities and good causes. Adnams was engaged in corporate social responsibility [CSR] well before the term was in common usage. From CSR it has proved only a short hop in recent years to formalising sustainability within the organisation's structure and purpose: using waste heat recovery systems from the brewery, for example, to heat the company-owned hotel, and switching to electric delivery vehicles. Its transition from plastic to glass bottles has also given Adnams considerable expertise in recyclable technologies, which it has been able to share with customers, raising Adnams' status as a supplier.

Lesson number two: it helps to have a supportive corporate culture that balances short-term imperatives with long-term ambitions. As the late, great Peter Drucker also put it, every global business problem and social issue is an opportunity in disguise.

Like Adnams, most small firms have larger firms as their customers, and often as their suppliers. As supply chains are subjected to increasing sustainability scrutiny, they will have little choice but to engage with this agenda if they are to win and retain business – especially if that business is won through commercial or government tenders.

Within larger firms sustainability is now routinely incorporated into corporate processes and structures, often overseen by teams of dedicated professionals. While still an independent business UK retailer Argos tasked an in-house sustainability team with developing new initiatives. In 2015 the company piloted a scheme badged as Gadget Trade-in, which enabled customers to trade in old mobile phones and thereby receive a discount on the purchase of a new one. The unwanted phones were sent away for dismantling, and the precious metal components recovered for recycling and sold on. Launched with an advertising fanfare, the scheme was well-received. Store staff got behind it enthusiastically: Gadget Trade-in increased customer footfall and showed the company in a good light. Unfortunately, the initiative never progressed beyond the pilot. Senior management attention shifted elsewhere and the project was relegated to the sidelines. Today Argos is owned by Sainsburys. Argos customers can still trade in their old phones and tablets – but only by post, and by going online. No longer prominently promoted, Gadget Trade-in, or Trade-in as it is now called, is a husk of its former self.

Lesson number three: it's comparatively easy to start something. Following through and maintaining the momentum is the hard bit. If you don't want to risk your staff growing cynical and your critics accusing you of greenwashing, the firm needs to be in it for the long haul.

New bedfellows

The Gadget-Trade-in project was developed by an in-house team, but in partnership with a specialist consultancy. Partnerships and alliances, both tight and loose, are a mechanism which many corporates are using to push sustainability initiatives forwards. Marks & Spencer had been in alliance for many years with Oxfam, as part of its Fair Trade initiative. Following the launch of Plan A in 2007, M&S widened the relationship to its clothing retail business, to help achieve the objective of 'zero to landfill'. The firm estimated that many millions of tonnes of unwanted M&S garments were being sent to landfill every year, and that this was simply unacceptable. Oxfam, in M&S's view, had the best facilities in the UK for sorting clothing into what could be resold through their 750 shops, what could be exported, and what could be recycled. Thus the Shwop scheme, which rewarded M&S customers for depositing unwanted 'pre-loved' clothing in store, for collection by Oxfam staff, was launched. In July 2022 the firm's website reported that since 2008 M&S and Oxfam Shwopping partnership had collected over 35 million items, contributing an estimated £23 million to Oxfam's global work.

Lesson number four: sustainability initiatives rarely happen in isolation. As the old saying goes, 'a problem shared is a problem halved'. The best, long-term solutions frequently arise out of deep, committed partnerships, where each party can play to its strengths.

Collaboration can assume unusual and unpredictable forms. Consumer goods giant Unilever is the world's largest producer of ice cream and ready-to-drink ice tea, the former requiring freezer storage and the latter chiller cabinets. In *Environmental debt*★, former Greenpeace Solutions Director Amy Larkin describes how in 2004 the company joined a new initiative, convened by the

United Nations and Greenpeace, called Refrigerants Naturally. Its aim was to replace the CFC and HFC refrigerant gases that were fracturing the ozone layer with environmentally friendly alternatives sponsored by Greenpeace. Not everyone in Unilever was happy about this. Not only did this mean working with an activist group which had opposed the firm on a number of fronts. It also meant sitting at the table with commercial rivals such as Coca-Cola and McDonalds on a cross-industry basis, to work towards a common purpose. The scale of the project was huge. Massive changes would be required across some of the most complex food supply chains in the world. It took five years and brought together the unlikely grouping of the UN, a campaigning NGO and competing corporations. Perhaps the most remarkable aspect of Refrigerants Natural was that two years into the project Pepsi-Cola joined, its representatives sitting next to those from Coca-Cola, to share their knowledge and devise common solutions. It worked because the scope of the initiative was strictly defined and the partners had more to gain from attaining a shared goal than to lose.

*See Amy Larkin, *Environmental debt*, Palgrave Macmillan, 2013

Lesson number five: the right partner in a sustainability initiative might not be the ideal partner, and you may have to overcome strong internal opposition to push it through. But who said leadership was easy?

In conclusion, much heat can be taken out of the hot potato that is sustainability if business leaders bear three things in mind.

First, governments and regulators will apply increasing pressure on companies to demonstrate their sustainability credentials through compliance and audit. Additional pressure will also probably come from industry peers and employees. In an age of social media and round-the-clock reporting there will be ever fewer places to conceal dirty laundry. It's best not to try.

Second, everyone has a different starting point in this particular journey. Reasonable people will acknowledge this and accept that for most businesses improving their credentials as good corporate citizens is a process, not an event. If critics or zealots make unrealistic demands, be prepared to challenge, not capitulate.

Third, the *direction* of travel is the most important element in this debate. After all, wouldn't most of us like to leave things in a better state than we found them?

©David Molian

In formulating this piece I am most grateful to my Cranfield colleagues Dr Rosina Watson and Emeritus Professor David Grayson for sharing their insights and research findings. The conclusions are my own.

FORCES DRIVING BUSINESSES TO EMBRACE SUSTAINABILITY

- *Current* employees – and that includes directors – will not want to be associated with a business which has an impaired reputation
- *Future* employees will not be attracted to such businesses: and we live in an age of shrinking working-age populations
- *Shareholders* will reconsider whether they wish to continue their ownership of companies with damaged brands
- *Customers* may elect the road of ethical boycotts
- *Suppliers* may decide that links to "bad" corporate citizens pose too great a commercial risk
- Perhaps most importantly, *good credentials* will move from being an order winner to being an order qualifier[3]

The internet age offers ever fewer places to hide from external scrutiny.

EXAMPLES AND CASE STUDIES

I think stories are the PDF files of human information. They are the vehicle we use for storing information, and the vehicle we use for sharing it. Stories are a universal format, like the PDF file.

(Rory Sutherland, VP Ogilvy, extracted from
a conversation with Steven Bartlett, 2022)

Most smaller firms actually serve business-to-business markets, and that composition of enterprises is reflected in participation on the Business Growth Programme. The cases and examples selected in this book are mostly – but not exclusively – direct-to-consumer businesses, on the basis that these brands are ones readers are most likely to know or to have come into contact with. You may even be a customer, but unaware of the story behind the business. The same principles which these cases illustrate, however, apply equally to organisations that do not sell direct to the end customer.

Our experience also challenges the prevailing myth that business growth is directly correlated with or confined to emerging and dynamic industry sectors. It is true that growth sectors such as IT, competitive sports and entertainment offer multiple entry points for ambitious entrepreneurs, but we have seen founders achieve remarkable success in what look like steady-state, unglamorous sectors, such as plumbing supplies and debt recovery. [For some surprising insights, we recommend readers to Business Growth Programme alumnus Jamie Waller's recent *Unsexy Business*]. There is no necessary equivalence between celebrity and making money.

A UNIQUE VANTAGE POINT

Because the Business Growth Programme [BGP] has been running since the 1980s, the programme directors have enjoyed the privileged access of witnessing the long-term success of some of Britain's best-performing gazelle businesses. By the time this book is published at least 5,000 businesses will have taken part in BGP and its stablemate programmes. A handful of pioneers joined the first BGP in 1988, which ran once a year. Within fifteen years the number of participants had grown to over 100, and the programme was run first twice, then three times per annum. As a consequence, we have improved our own first-hand knowledge of what it's like to grow a business! Most of those forming the team delivering the programmes that comprise the BGP portfolio today are former participants who are no longer involved in the day-to-day management of their companies, or who have sold up and are now mentoring the next generation of ambitious founders. Thanks to them, and to all we have worked with, we have never stopped learning.

Some businesses have attended BGP more than once: outdoor adventure specialist GoApe, for example, has taken part twice. On each occasion the founders were faced with a critical decision and used the programme and the insights from their fellow participants to create a plan for the company's next stage of development. The lifecycle of most businesses that stay the course is punctuated by a series of forks in the road, when the founders have to make significant choices that will shape the future. It may be a cliché, but growing a business really is a marathon, not a sprint, and you are more likely to succeed if you plan for the long haul:

Figure I.1 depicts the four types of growth journey [GJ] featured in this book:

- The first, GJ 1, is the route most commonly travelled. The business grows organically, financed through its own earnings and bank debt, and value is realised through a sale in full either to a trade buyer or to a private equity house. The *Witan Jardine, Pacific Direct* and *Aerospares 2000* cases are examples of this type.

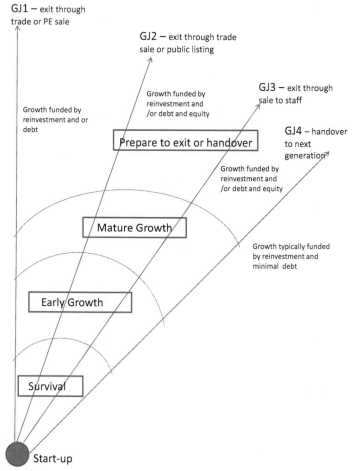

GJ1 – exit through trade or PE sale

GJ2 – exit through trade sale or public listing

GJ3 – exit through sale to staff

GJ4 – handover to next generation

Growth funded by reinvestment and or debt

Growth funded by reinvestment and /or debt and equity

Prepare to exit or handover

Growth funded by reinvestment and /or debt and equity

Mature Growth

Growth typically funded by reinvestment and minimal debt

Early Growth

Survival

Start-up

Figure I.1 Growth Journeys Illustrated by Case Studies.[4]

- The second, GJ 2, is a variation on the first type. The business grows partly through reinvested earnings, but more commonly through a broader range of debt financing and outside equity. It is sold in part or in full either to a trade buyer or via a public listing on a stock market. The *Moonpig* and *Hotel Chocolat* cases are examples.

- The third type, GJ 3, consists of growth through reinvestment and bank debt, and culminates in a sale to staff. *GoApe* illustrates this route, which is relatively uncommon but growing in popularity.
- GJ 4 refers to family-controlled businesses, which are passed from one generation to the next. They tend to follow a conservative financing policy, funding their growth mainly through reinvestment. *Belvoir Cordials* and *Ravensden Plc* are illustrative cases.

FUNDING THE JOURNEY

It is worth making clear that this book has little to say about raising external [equity] finance in these journeys to growth. The Moonpig story, in which the business was funded by successive rounds of angel and institutional [private] equity, is something of an exception. The omission of such a discussion is deliberate:

First, because only a tiny proportion of owner-managed businesses are financed through institutional, or even business angel, investment. For example, Beauhurst, which closely tracks private equity investment, reported that between January and November 2021, 552 UK companies announced their first round of private equity or venture capital funding. Roughly half a billion pounds was raised in that period, and half of that at a very early stage ["seed" funding] in the life of those businesses. Beaufort described these figures as impressive. Even if ten times that number of businesses had received such investment this would still be a minute fraction of the business population: the Office for National Statistics reported that between March 2020 and March 2021, 753,168 new businesses were created. Business founders are far more likely to encounter private equity at the point of exit, as we shall see.

Second, very few small businesses, however ambitious, meet the growth criteria for this kind of external investment. Institutional capital seeks businesses that can scale rapidly and build value that can be crystallised, i.e. turned into cash through a sale, within a relatively short period, typically seven to ten years. It takes many ambitious businesses that long just to establish and build a profitable niche position in their market.

Third, most participants on courses such as the Business Growth Programme are wary of outside equity finance. Either they view external investors as a threat to their operational autonomy, or they have heard too many scare stories of owners who have lost control of their businesses to venture capital investors. Sometimes both reasons apply.

THE ORGANISATION OF THIS BOOK: FIVE CRITICAL CHALLENGES TO GROWTH

The **first three** chapters of this book address both operational and strategic barriers to business growth. They focus on the existing state of the ambitious business, and encourage you to take a deep dive under the bonnet, so to speak, to fine-tune the engine and get your business vehicle in the best possible shape. They introduce the analytical approaches that have underpinned the Business Growth Programme, to navigate the obstacles that hinder successful growth. Much of what we have learnt comes from close observation and documentation of what businesses that are outstanding in their sectors have achieved, as well as mistakes they have made along the way, and how these can be avoided.

- **Chapter 1** looks at the markets you choose to operate in now and in the future, and why it makes sense to build a business in a niche that offers protection from the competition. A major cause of business failure is the pursuit of seemingly attractive, but unrelated opportunities too early on. All too often these turn out to be markets the founder does not really understand, and constitute too big a stretch from the core business activity.
- **Chapter 2** deals with finance. Unless they have a background in finance or accounting, most business founders

have only a sketchy understanding of financial reporting metrics, processes and systems. In most cases, an enhanced understanding of how money flows in and out of the business, and how that performance is measured, enables you to make incremental and even dramatic improvements. The systems and processes which underpin the business need to be solid, repeatable and dependable to support the firm's expansion.

- **Chapter 3** concerns the changes in the roles played by the founder as the business develops and how his or her management style needs to adapt. We introduce the Artisan-Hero-Meddler-Strategist model which describes the behavioural changes necessary to create a business that runs independently of the founder/owner. This personal journey is integral to building the value that will make the firm an asset that stands on its own two feet, creating options for the future.

Chapters 4 and 5 are concerned with the more mature stages of the business and how it reaches its full potential – or at least as far as the founder/owner wants to take it. The common theme is what is needed to build value in the business, and how that depends in turn on the scalability of the enterprise and the founder/owner's capacity to change and adapt.

- **Chapter 4** probes the basis on which you compete in your market. Sustainable growth is closely related to your ability to show how your business is better or different from the competition in a way that is relevant to your marketplace. Rarely can a small business compete purely on price, so growth hinges on finding other ways to create value in the eyes of your customers.
- **Chapter 5** has two themes: maximising that creation of value through scaling up, and crystallising that value. In the first part, we analyse how successful owners have pursued either evolutionary or revolutionary strategies to transform

their businesses as attractive entities with independent value. In the second part, we describe the ways that owners exchange assets for cash through different forms of sale, depending on their personal priorities and preferences.

At the end of each chapter you will find:

- Suggested accelerants, beartraps and blockers, as described above
- A summary of the key features of each challenge and how they are overcome
- References for further reading on themes that you might like to follow up

NOTES

1 According to *Sifted*, an authoritative publication on the European technology sector, at mid-2022, 35% of UK unicorn businesses [companies valued at $1 bn or more] were founded by immigrants. It's a very small sample, but indicative nonetheless.

2 As an indicator, according to the most recent *Global Entrepreneurship Monitor* total early-stage [active] entrepreneurial activity in the UK was 11.5%, compared to 6.9% for Germany, 7.7% for France and 16.5% for the US. How many of these British businesses actually fulfil their ambitions is harder to quantify.

3 *Forbes* magazine, May 2023, reported research from the Vlerick Business School that investing in the environmental, social and governance [ESG] initiatives that underpin sustainability practice tends to make small firms more resilient. On average, an 11% increase in small firms' ESG performance decreases their credit risk by 3.5%. The researchers concluded that sustainability-driven SMEs were more resilient to large shocks, making them more creditworthy.

4 In general a relatively small number of high-growth owner-managed/ entrepreneurial businesses are financed through external institutional capital, such as venture capital funds. The publicity received by the tech. sector tends to obscure this.

FURTHER READING

For a comprehensive overview of the business case for sustainability, see *The Sustainable Business Handbook: a guide to becoming more innovative, resilient and successful* [Kogan Page, 2022], Grayson, Coulter and Lee. A fair number of UK organisations – at the time of writing, over 1,000 – have gone down the route of certifying as a B [benefit] – corporation [B-corp], a kitemark of good citizenship. For an overview, visit www.bcorporation.net.

As an example of the risk to a business's reputation if it fails to live up to the standards expected of B-Corp status, see www.theguardian.com/business/2022/dec/01/brewdog-loses-its-ethical-b-corp-certificate), and reports from the BBC www.youtube.com/watch?v=XamxzvGm8YQ and Sky News www.youtube.com/watch?v=w9tDi2ne8i0

For insights into UK fast-growth businesses financed by external [venture capital], see the full range of reports regularly produced by data specialist Beauhurst: www.beauhurst.com.

CHALLENGE TO GROWTH NUMBER ONE: STICK TO THE KNITTING

OR THE ART OF NOT SELLING THINGS YOU DON'T REALLY UNDERSTAND TO PEOPLE YOU'VE NEVER MET

Belvoir [pronounced beaver] Fruit Farms is one of the UK's best-known and most successful domestic soft drinks producers, based at the family-owned farm in Leicestershire. Today the company sells more than 40 different varieties of its fruit cordials and carbonated drinks[1] through supermarkets, farm shops, delicatessens and wholesale distributors both in the UK and overseas, even as far as Australia. In addition to the elderflower grown on its own acres, the business is supplied by other local farms and has its own newly expanded bottling plant.

Like so many success stories, the company began life at the kitchen table. The Manners family produced elderflower cordials for their own consumption and as gifts for friends. In 1984 what was more or less a hobby developed into a modest business, with the sale of just over 1,000 bottles to local fine food stores and farm shops. In response to demand, sales tripled the following year and soon afterwards the company produced raspberry and lemon cordials to supplement its staple elderflower. And so the business steadily progressed. By 1992 nine flavours were being sold. Five years later Belvoir developed sparkling, ready-to-drink variants of its most popular lines and in 1998 went organic with its elderflower variant. Throughout this time the company

DOI: 10.4324/9781003410614-2

positioned its products as premium-quality soft drinks, aimed at the adult market.

By 2000 the son of the founders, Peverel Manners, had left his job in the City to join the business as Managing Director. He saw opportunities everywhere and was eager to seize them, without compromising the reputation of the Belvoir brand. After he took part in the Business Growth Programme, and had drawn up a plan for growth, we went to visit him on the farm and to tour the production plant. In a corner of the factory we noticed some dusty bottles bearing a label very different from the elegantly-scripted design on the bottles going through the lines. These neglected-looking bottles were branded Beaver, and the brightly coloured labels duly featured an animated beaver, drawn in cartoon style. Out of curiosity, we picked one up to take a closer look. "Ah yes," said Pev ruefully. "That was our brief foray into the children's market. We don't do that anymore!"

The soft drinks market has a very specific set of rules.

The biggest and best-known players, Coca-Cola and its rival Pepsi, have been in business for well over a hundred years. For the first few decades of their existence, these companies just stuck to their core business and to selling their core products. If you look closely at how these businesses have been so successful, two factors stand out: the strength of their flagship brands, and their networks of distribution. It's been said that there is virtually nowhere on the planet where you are more than a few metres away from an outlet or a vending machine from which you can purchase a Coke. It's an exaggeration, but not by much. What you *won't* find is a range of hundreds of variants of Coca-Cola or Pepsi-Cola. Instead, you will find comparatively few variants of both products, sold in lots of different sizes and packaging formats, designed for convenience and to promote consumption. Of course, the two brand owners each have a big portfolio of other brands, but when it comes to the core for which they are famous they put their development efforts into promoting the brand and creating new opportunities to purchase via expanded distribution channels and new pack types. Business innovation can take many forms and the recipe for sales success in this industry seems no less potent than the secret formulae of their respective syrups. Distribution, availability and brand focus are the trump cards to play for sustainable growth in soft drinks.

INTRODUCTION: WHY NOT ALL OPPORTUNITIES ARE EQUAL

People *start* businesses because they see an opportunity. They *grow* businesses because they see additional opportunities to build on what they have started. As a general rule, when we talk to ambitious business owners about their ideas for growth they tell us that they are overwhelmed by opportunities to expand what they are already doing. Opportunities are everywhere: the problem is not finding them, but assembling the resources to exploit them. Unfortunately this abundance of choice too often creates two kinds of problem:

- people who are naturally attuned to pursuing opportunities often tend to go after these at random, chasing after what others will label – if they are feeling generous – as pet projects. And not only are business owners deeply attached to their pet projects they are also notoriously reluctant to abandon them, long after it has become clear to everyone else that they are a waste of the company's time and resources.
- pet projects are a diversion from the core of the business. As has been famously said, in business the main thing is to focus on the main thing.

In this chapter, we explain exactly why such diversions occur, why they are so damaging to a business's development, and how balancing the opportunistic instinct with strategic thinking can keep a business on the right growth trajectory. Choose the right opportunities, for the right reasons and in the right order, and you will save your business time and money, and create value faster.

TAKING THE EYE OFF THE BALL

Many business founders will admit they are prone to distraction, and their staff tend to agree. When it comes to choosing how to grow the business, this tendency can often produce adverse results, taking the company into markets which it doesn't properly understand. The problem is neatly illustrated by that old marketers' favourite, the Ansoff matrix (Figure 1.1).

On the vertical axis is the market in which the business currently operates, or might potentially operate in; and on the horizontal axis the products or services the business currently sells, or might potentially sell. The result is to carve the arena of play into four quadrants, each representing a choice of strategy. Going clockwise, from bottom left:

- **Market penetration** is selling more of what you currently do to existing customers and others like them

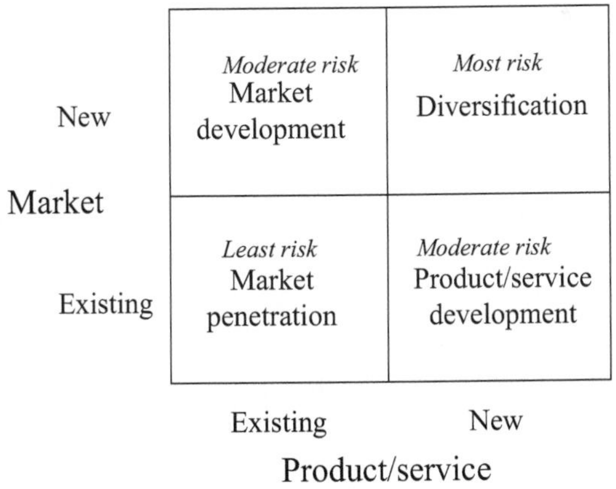

New	*Moderate risk* Market development	*Most risk* Diversification
Market		
Existing	*Least risk* Market penetration	*Moderate risk* Product/service development
	Existing	New
	Product/service	

Figure 1.1 The Ansoff Matrix [modified].
Source: *Growing Your Business: A Handbook for Ambitious Owner-Managers,* Routledge, 2008

- **Market development** is taking the existing portfolio of goods or services into a new market
- **Diversification** is selling new things to a new market[s]
- **Product/Service development** is expanding what you currently do, to sell to existing customers

THE BUSINESS OF RISK

The matrix not only lays out the strategic choices for business growth. It also clarifies the *degree of risk* the business takes in making those choices. In the early stages of a company's life, market penetration is almost always the strategy of least risk. It's not hard to see why. The business is focusing its efforts on selling more of what it currently does – and understands – to customers who already know the supplier they are trading with. The firm has established terms of trade and lines of supply. Across the firm there are likely to be good informal relationships between the staff and their counterparts in its customer base. If there's a problem, the chances are it can be resolved fairly quickly and informally before it escalates, because a degree of trust has been built up. And if relations are good, happy customers are usually willing to provide testimonials and case studies that evidence the value they receive. Given that many smaller firms have larger firms as their customers, there are typically unexplored opportunities to sell to other potential buyers within the same customer, especially if that customer has multiple sites or business divisions: the most cost-effective means of doing this is usually by simply asking for referrals or recommendations, and making this a key measure of sales performance.

In short, there is often a veritable mountain of untapped opportunities to increase sales within the existing customer base before turning to others, and this strategy carries the least commercial risk. On the Business Growth Programme we call it *squeezing the lemon*.

IDEAS FOR BETTER LEMON-SQUEEZING
[EXTRACTED FROM DAVID MOLIAN'S BLOG]

In my many years of working with independent businesses I've learned the value of lemon-squeezing.... I use "lemon-squeezing" to describe getting more value out of your existing business and existing customer base. And, yes, it's based on a cooking observation.

Most people, when they add lemon juice to a dish, will tend to do the following:

Take a lemon. Slice it. Squeeze one half – partially. Discard. Take second, unsqueezed half, wrap in clingfilm (this is optional), and place in back of fridge. Open fridge two weeks later to discover mouldering piece of lemon and discard, unsqueezed.

Well, that's how it works when I'm in the kitchen.

My observation is that this is also how it works for a lot of businesses. You extract a certain amount of business from your customers, just enough for present purposes. Then you put them in cold storage and when you go back to them, they've gone sour on you. Sounds familiar? All the evidence suggests that most successful independently-owned and managed businesses grow through business development: they sell more of their existing products and services to their existing customers, and others who are like them. In other words, they become better and better at squeezing lemons.

Over the years I've been assembling hint and tips, based on anecdotes from entrepreneurs I've worked with. Here are a few choice ones for you to share in *your* organisation:

1. **Assign responsibility for lemon-squeezing as a priority to one person, who can look at opportunities across the organisation and across the customer base.** One participant in a 2004 Cranfield Programme described his experience of putting this into place even before the programme was finished:

   > "I know from analysis in the [Cranfield] market research database that our competition claim to get at least 60% of their income from existing customers. We get about 35%. We are missing a trick!

We've taken two key initiatives:

1) Moved a key member of staff into a role specifically aimed at squeezing lemons. He will work as a 'Consultant', offering to help customers do a health check on their systems. The objective is to make them feel looked after and not feel pressurised by a salesman. Already the customers are beginning to buy additional services.
2) Cross-sell. With very minor modifications, our essentially vertical market products can be adapted to provide benefits to the other market sectors: e.g. our charity customers can benefit from our document management product. Our Engineering customers will welcome our CRM solutions once we change the terminology in the software."

Subsequently he [the business founder/owner] told me that they'd generated at least £100k net extra from these two exercises.

2. **Move towards a key account mgt (KAM) structure, with a plan for growing major individual accounts.** Here's what happened at market research business Cobalt-Sky (Cranfield BGP 2002):

   > "I got our sales director to set up the KAM. He identified our key clients, bought some consultancy time from a sales person, and now spends most of his time working with our main clients building relationships. We've stopped looking at competing on price and are working with a core group of people who are happy to pay our fees in return for great service. We've got the whole company behind this, as it's the work they do that proves the sales offering: it is "what it says on the tin".

"The nice thing is that everyone is involved. We had an instance where a customer asked one of our people for a set of data in a specific format. Our chap queried this and it turned out he was looking for a certain type of software, and we actually did something similar, albeit in a different department. Our guy then convinced him to look at our product – it's still ongoing, but the main lesson is that our people are now awake to potential sales, outside of their normal work.

"We are also getting a lot of good feedback from our clients about how they enjoy the contact outside of project-specific meetings, and it's quite unique in our industry.

"It's very hard to pin down how much work has resulted from this, but since BGP (which obviously takes the credit!) our sales have grown by 34% and profits by 134%."

3. **Make it easy to buy through creating options.** Peter Wood, a Cranfield BGPer from the Jan 2005 programme, contacted me with a great example of this approach. His firm, Wychwood Water Systems, specialises in water treatment. Peter took an enquiry from someone who was thinking of buying a second-hand water purification system, maintained and serviced by Wychwood. The enquirer had been to view the system, saw Wychwood's contact details on the equipment, and phoned for a chat.

Peter takes over the story: "Having listened to him I advised him that the equipment was too large for his needs and at the price asked was too expensive. He also told me that they had limited capital funds and, if possible, would prefer to rent a solution. Our preferred option is always to sell new equipment. So I made an appointment to visit him, look at the application and meet his MD."

Peter also spoke to fellow BGPer Saul Pitaluga, a director of capital equipment finance house Tower Leasing. In the Wychwood quotation for the system were the terms from Tower for three-and five-year leasing arrangements.

"The end result," says Peter," was a happy client, an order worth almost £20k for Wychwood and a leasing agreement for Tower. This is the first time we have ever actively promoted leasing. But obviously we will not hesitate to do so again.

"The lesson seems to be that, when offered leasing terms, the client is no longer focussed on the capital cost of the project. The capital value of this project actually came in at nearly double what we thought it would be!"

4. **Test your pre-conceived ideas about customer price resistance.** Forward Press produce bespoke books of children's poetry, aimed at the schools market. MD Ian Walton described how he suggested squeezing the lemon by adding an uplift to the postage charged on each order. His fellow director was unsure that this would work, but suggested instead that they increased the cover price by £1/per copy. This has been done and encountered no price resistance at all, netting the business an immediate uplift in net profit of £35k/month, recurring.

©David Molian 2023

MARKET DEVELOPMENT: KNOW YOUR CUSTOMER AND WHY YOU WIN THEIR BUSINESS

Having survived the start-up and early stages, the business is almost certainly on its way to establishing a niche position in the market. If you are winning business consistently, there is bound to be a good fit between why customers buy from you, and your ability to stand out from the competition. It's very unlikely to be solely on the basis of price. Selling an undifferentiated product at low prices that undercut the competition normally leads to unsustainably low margins and challenges from other suppliers. Larger competitors, with bigger purchasing muscle, are better-placed to win a price war. In this kind of David and Goliath battle, the smart money is invariably with Goliath.

By contrast, we have observed three enduring types of competitive advantage that enhance the growth of ambitious owner-managed businesses:

- the capacity to innovate
- fostering internal efficiencies
- the ability to inspire and retain customer loyalty

FOOD FOR THOUGHT #3

Hotel Chocolat is one of the UK's outstanding retail success stories. In 2003 the business opened its first store in Watford and by 2016 had grown large enough to list as a public company on the London Stock Exchange. At mid-year 2022 the company had grown to over 100 shops in the UK and some 33 in Japan. Walk around any Hotel Chocolat outlet and you quickly get a sense of what this business is all about: affordable luxury. A customer can spend £10, £20 or £100, buy a single bar or a de luxe chocolate box, a treat for oneself or a gift for loved ones. The range and variety of chocolate goods on sale are limited only by the imagination of the staff and the company's founders, Angus Thirlwell and Peter Harris. Innovation is everywhere – and by a relentless focus on bringing new ideas to market, Hotel Chocolat has transformed the purchase of chocolate from a mainly seasonal habit with high points such as Christmas and Easter to an all-year-round consumer trend.

Source: company store inspection

THE VIRTUE OF KEEPING IT SIMPLE

Internal efficiencies are what make a company easy to do business with. These are the firms that don't keep you waiting endlessly on the phone, that respond to your queries promptly, and deal with any hiccups or complaints efficiently and effectively. They fulfil their promises. Businesses possessing these qualities often stand in marked contrast to their larger rivals. If your company makes transactions easy, customers will not only return but are unlikely to baulk at paying a premium for exemplary service.

That said, keeping things simple is often easier to pay lip service to than to maintain. Another of the UK's successful high-growth firms, outdoor adventure specialist GoApe, regularly audits its customer experience. Ease of online booking is crucial to ensuring a high volume of customers in peak operating months. As the business has grown, so has the sophistication of its IT infrastructure, as you might expect. Unfortunately, what might seem a neat solution from an internal systems perspective can unintentionally translate into over-complexity from the user's point of view. What triggered a now regular process of review at GoApe was the discovery that the two clicks a customer once needed to make a booking had ballooned into seven steps. Once unearthed, this was quickly rectified, but a valuable lesson had been learned: making things complicated is easy. Keeping things simple for the customer requires constant vigilance. A whole new industry, that of "mystery shopping", has grown up, which records and maps the experience of transacting with a company from the perspective of the customer.

Inspiring and retaining customer loyalty is essentially a product of two things: providing reasons for the customer to return, and offering exemplary service. Through relevant innovation and by making your business easy to transact with, you increase the odds of both things happening.

FINDING NEW CUSTOMERS WHO ARE JUST LIKE THE OLD ONES

If the existing customer base cannot support the business founder's ambitions to grow in the short or medium term, it's only a short step to directing the sales and marketing effort towards other customers who have the same needs. In many cases, you already know who these potential customers are. Their names have come up in conversation internally, with your salesforce, or externally, in conversations with your current customers.

Often the main obstacle to selling to new customers is that there are no systems in place for capturing that information, despite there being numerous software systems designed for this purpose. When this happens, it's an early warning sign that the business can no longer be managed on an ad hoc, informal basis, and needs to move to a more structured mode of operation.

However, to make a success of expanding your reach, you first need to have in-depth knowledge of who your customers are and why they buy from you. That is one of the best reasons for seeking initially to sell more of what you currently produce to your existing customers, to improve your understanding of who they are and to embed that knowledge within the business.

LOOKING TO ADJACENCIES FOR OPPORTUNITIES TO GROW

To revert to the Ansoff matrix in Figure 1.1, the quadrants next to the Market Penetration box – selling existing products/services to new markets, and new products/services to existing markets – are frequently referred to as *adjacencies*. Selling to these quadrants is, or should be, a relatively low-risk strategy for growing the business, because only one new factor at a time is being introduced into the mix. New distribution channels or routes to market are frequently the best means of setting out your stall of existing products/services in front of new prospects. When Hotel Chocolat took part in the Business Growth Programme in 2000, it was essentially a mail-order operation, selling delivered products under the ChocExpress brand through catalogues and online. The founders, Angus Thirlwell and Peter Harris, felt that their opportunities to grow were constrained by consumer buying patterns: research suggested that 50% of potential customers would only ever consider using in-store purchase of chocolates for gifts for themselves or other people. At the same time, the duo had concluded that the ChocExpress brand undersold the quality of the company's products. After nearly two years of painstaking consumer research, Angus and Peter rebranded the business and opened their first Hotel Chocolat store in Watford. The rest, as they say, is history.

Expanding a business's product offer is frequently prompted by the appetite of existing customers for more: "What else do you do?" Belvoir's farm shop and fine food customers had a well-developed sense of what *their* customers would buy. Two years after the first cases of elderflower cordial were sold, Belvoir added raspberry and lemon variants to the range, which served as complements and alternatives to elderflower. For Belvoir, this was a manageable expansion that would not strain the company's resources. If it was successful, the business could do more, at its own pace [in fact it took another ten years before Belvoir took its first sparkling, ready-to-drink product to market]. From the perspective of a small retailer, it makes sense both to look to trusted suppliers for new products that keep customers coming back and to limit the number of suppliers they deal with to prevent procurement from getting overly complex. As far as the consumer is concerned, he or she gets more choice and variety. In this scenario, everyone wins.

THE DIVERSIFICATION TRAP

The biggest risk that some ambitious businesses are tempted to take is premature diversification: jumping too early into that top-right quadrant of the Ansoff matrix. We characterised this earlier as selling things you don't really understand to people you have never met – arguably an extreme description, but nonetheless a true one. Stepping out of your zone of competence too soon is an effective way to stunt the growth of a promising business. Risk surrounds the company on all fronts:

- Combining a new assortment of products/services with a new target market places a huge strain on all areas of the business. If you provide goods, you will probably need to source new raw materials or semi-finished components, which those responsible for procurement are not familiar with. If you provide services, you will need to overhaul the training of existing staff or hire new people. Your sales and marketing people will have to educate themselves on the dynamics of the new market and the way in which customers buy – and understand a whole new set of competitors. Your accounts staff will almost certainly encounter different terms of trade and service requirements. In the past, the business had developed a grasp of the credit risks and cash flow associated with its customer base. That knowledge may or may not serve as a guide to new financial risks. In short, everything becomes a lot more complicated and almost always more uncertain.

- As the business's resources become stretched, there's a danger that you neglect your established customers while not fully serving the new ones.
- And you may well find yourself revisiting the kind of challenge that you first encountered at start-up: 'I've never heard of you, your brand or your company: why should I buy from you?' Does your business have a compelling answer?

If there are so many strong arguments against diversifying too early on in the life of a business, why does it happen? Our conversations with business founders/owners have revealed two main causes. First, many entrepreneurs are by their own admission prone to distraction and the excitement of 'new stuff': they are too easily bored. Second is the lure of the big deal, the great opportunity that can change the fortunes of the business in one giant leap. The grass, alas, is not always greener:

FOOD FOR THOUGHT #4

In the early days of its existence, the business that is now Hotel Chocolat was offered a contract with a large UK supermarket. The deal was to provide a range of chocolate gift items under the supermarket's own brand label, to be stocked across the country. With a single order, Hotel Chocolat would be catapulted into the next league. The dream, however, rapidly became a nightmare.

> *From dealing with individual customers who paid as they placed their orders, the business found itself frantically servicing one giant client which ordered as it chose, paid in significant arrears and operated with minimal lead times. Matters came to a head when the chocolate Easter bunnies supplied by the company slowly melted under the hot lights inside the supermarket's display cabinets – against Hotel Chocolat's advice – and the customer then refused to pay, claiming that the products were made of inferior ingredients.*
>
> *That was the company's first and last venture into the supermarket sector.*
>
> Source: Cranfield Hotel Chocolat case study

IT TAKES TIME TO BUILD A SUSTAINABLE, DEFENSIBLE NICHE

The following is a version of an article first published in *The Cambridge Marketing Review*, Issue 5, and explores at greater length what it takes to build a sustainable, defensive market niche:

The focus, however, in this article is on marketing and so let me state a general assertion about what it takes to succeed as an entrepreneurial business, by which I mean a high-growth business that creates enduring value for the founder and other shareholders. *The foundation stone of every such business that I know is the identification and occupation of a sustainable, defensible market niche.* This applies across the board: whether the business is business-to-business, business-to-consumer, whether it is bricks and mortar or virtual, domestically focused or born global, high tech, low tech or no tech. For entrepreneurs who have given this little thought before, I pose the question as starkly as possible: in what way is your business better or different? Some can answer that question immediately, citing a specific advantage or set of attributes which are impossible or difficult for competitors to replicate. [The potency of this competitive advantage is frequently overestimated, but the qualities of over-optimism and mild self-delusion are vital in getting entrepreneurs through difficult times in the lives of their businesses.] However, most entrepreneurs struggle for that elusive USP [unique selling proposition], some because they can't quite articulate it but they know that it's there, and others because they haven't [yet] developed clear, identifiable points of difference.

The importance of niche derives from two self-evident facts of business life. The first is that starting *and sustaining* a new venture is inherently difficult, and most businesses will fail within the first ten years of their existence. Conversely, those that survive will have a disproportionately greater chance of surviving the *next* ten years. Unless there is something distinctive about what you are selling, why should someone a) buy from you in the first place; and b) continue to buy from you in the future? The salience of this is underscored by the second fact of business life, namely that – in advanced economies at any rate – most markets suffer from over-supply, and competition is rife. There are, of course, exceptions to this. The early adopters of embryonic technologies – PC software and mobile phones in the 1980s, for example – were prepared to put up with bug-ridden, crash-prone programmes or carry bricks around with them because they were desperate to get their hands on a scarce resource. But the early and late majorities wisely held off until they got something that worked reliably and conveniently. And in the shake-out between early and later-stage adoption, numerous suppliers went to the wall.[2]

Finding and building a niche

Some important implications flow from the central importance of finding and building a niche position:

Entrepreneurs frequently underestimate how long it takes to establish their market position. Outside information technology markets, which have timescales all of their own, it generally takes longer, and costs more than the founders anticipate. Pret à Manger spent four years getting the first outlet right before opening their second. Hotel Chocolat went through three brand incarnations and nearly fifteen years of experimentation before perfecting today's extremely successful business model. Business-to-business operations are no different. Our questioning of founders who participate in the Cranfield Business Growth Programme suggests that it takes *at least seven* *years* before the typical owner-manager fully understands the markets he or she serves and what makes their business tick.

Avoiding premature diversification

The corollary of the previous point is that many promising ventures never fulfil their potential because the founders dilute their focus too early in the life of the business. They are enticed or seduced by other opportunities and find themselves drawn into a position where they both neglect their core customer base *and* cannot give sufficient time, attention and resource to their new target market. All customers, however, are not created equal and what looks on the surface like a greener pasture is all too often a far more difficult and challenging environment than the business owner envisaged.

For the small business owner, the classic trap of this kind is that afforded by the contract with the big customer, especially a major retailer. Cobra Beer, a business which attended the Business Growth Programme in the late 1990s, focused for nearly a decade on the tandoori restaurant sector. The company built their brand, extended their product range, and secured a loyal consumer franchise in what was a semi-protected niche. Only when their roots were deep did they migrate to new channels, first into off-licences, then into supermarkets. By the time the brand hit the retailers' shelves Cobra was sufficiently established to deal on terms that were acceptable to the business; and if, for whatever reason, the brand had been delisted, the loss of one big account would not jeopardise the business as a whole.

"Making money is simple, but it isn't easy"

Our surveys suggest that as many as nine out of ten businesses that grow successfully consciously pursue niche-building as their number one market strategy. They have taken on board the value of the maxim quoted above, attributable, I believe, to John Bloom of Rolls Razor fame. While he may no longer be a household name, his invaluable aperçu survives. Like so many basic truths of business life, it is easy to grasp but hard to live by. The arithmetic of making money is disarmingly simple. The mechanics are not. In this context, the enemies of success are unnecessary complexity and ill-considered risk.

Extract by permission of *The Cambridge Marketing Review*

ACCELERANTS

The most powerful accelerant for market growth is that which we have frequently referred to, identifying and occupying a defensible market niche. As described above, Cobra Beer's market entry sector was the tandoori or "Indian" restaurant segment: numbering around 8,000 in the UK of the late 1980s, this sector was too small to attract the serious attention of Britain's big beer brands. They were far more interested in the much bigger mainstream markets of pubs, restaurants, hotels and off-licences. But curry houses formed a perfect size for a new entrant, with a proposition designed specifically to complement this cuisine: a beer that was less gassy than a conventional lager, and thus able to be consumed in larger quantities [more curry could also be eaten!]. At the same time, this sector was big enough to scale up the business for the first ten years or so of its life, and to build a significant brand, strengthening its bargaining position when it came eventually to selling into supermarkets and off-licences.

The ability to command a price premium because what you offer is better or different. Money is the fuel that powers the business. Better margins – as we discuss in the next chapter – translate into more firepower for reinvestment and improved performance.

How you reward the salesforce: getting the balance right between hunters and farmers. If your salesforce are incentivised chiefly to recruit new customers, that's what they will do. When business owners express concern at the rate of customer 'churn' in the business, investigation normally reveals that existing customers have been neglected in the pursuit of new ones. The root cause in most cases is an imbalance between what we describe as *hunters* and *farmers*. The typical salesperson is driven by the excitement of landing new business: that's the hunting instinct. Once that business is secured, the hunter is on the lookout for the next sales opportunity. Farmers, on the other hand, are customer-facing staff motivated by the longer-term challenge of retaining and growing existing accounts and building the relationships necessary to achieve this. In its early days, a business tends to be dominated by hunters, since customer acquisition is critical to survival. As the business matures, the balance between the two types needs to be under constant review. Hunters will deliver customers, farmers will keep them, and they need to be rewarded on a different basis.

There's an overwhelming financial case as well. The weight of research evidence suggests that to acquire a new customer it can easily cost as much as four times as to hold on to a current one.

BEARTRAPS AND BLOCKERS

You've probably got the message already, but when it comes to market strategy the single biggest beartrap is diversifying from the core too early. Distractions are all around and the 'biscuit tin' of opportunity is rarely empty. Unfortunately, this kind of tempting snacking is almost always bad both for you and the business.

Over-reliance on a single route to market. iViewCameras, a promising start-up in the CCTV market, had its wings clipped too early when the cost of marketing quadrupled almost overnight. The original business opportunity arose in the early 2000s when the price of domestic and commercial CCTV systems fell dramatically. The company enjoyed initial success through selling online via Google, but this was virtually the company's sole route to market. The entry of new competitors saw a huge spike in advertising and search ranking rates, which translated into a vast increase in the cost of sales. As a small business, iViewCameras lacked the bargaining power of its bigger rivals. It had no alternative shop window to reach sales prospects, and a shortage of add-ons and upgrades to offer previous purchasers. The firm no longer exists.

Creeping complexity. Like a garden, a growing business needs constant weeding. Unnecessary complexity has a tendency to grow of its own accord. At regular intervals, the founder needs to replicate the customer's interaction with the business – or hire the services of a mystery shopper – to spot and root out needless processes that are making it harder for the customer to do business with you.

Lack of accountability on the part of the founder/ owner. In a big business, there are multiple checks and balances that constrain the power of those at the top to act. While there are well-publicised exceptions to this rule of thumb, such as Enron in the US and Carillion in the UK, these *are* exceptions to the rule and stand out because of this. Big firms are normally subject to well-defined corporate governance and the scrutiny of shareholders and other stakeholders. In an owner-managed business, where the founder[s] typically controls 100% of the shares, there is frequently no one to challenge the boss. Without boundaries, that freedom can be both a burden and a liability. Either the boss needs to initiate some process of internal challenge to their thinking – which is inherently difficult – or find an external mechanism for doing so. When we ask people their reasons for wanting to attend the Business Growth Programme, we are used to hearing founders tell us that they need an informed outside view.

SUMMARY

This first chapter has concentrated on your firm's market development strategy. At the core of every business is the ability to serve and retain customers. As your business expands, the balance between the relentless pursuit of opportunity and the need to think strategically has to change:

- Beware pet projects that consume the business's time and resources. However appealing they are to the founders/ owners, short-term diversions are the wrong opportunities to chase after. Be honest with yourself and ruthless in terminating projects that lead nowhere.

- Avoid price wars. You may have entered the market through competing on price, but being the cheapest is unlikely to sustain your growth in the longer term. Bigger competitors will always have a cost advantage: they have superior buying power and greater economies of scale and scope. In a price war, the little guy loses.
- In developing your market, use the enduring competitive advantages of the smaller, agile business:

  - the capacity to innovate
  - the fostering of internal efficiencies
  - the ability to inspire and retain customer loyalty

- Before expanding your reach, know exactly who your customers are and why they buy from you. What is it that makes you special in their eyes?
- Think niche, niche, niche. Use market adjacencies to broaden and deepen your position in the market – after market penetration, it's the strategy of least risk.
- Above all, avoid the early diversification trap, however tempting.
- Hunters will win you customers. Farmers will keep them. Review the balance periodically.
- Complexity is not your friend. Without constant vigilance, a business gets more complicated, less efficient and less profitable.

NOTES

1 Cordials are concentrated syrups; carbonated products are ready-to-drink products.
2 A great example is provided in the director's cut of *Blade Runner*, which features advertising signage for hot technology brands of the '80s – such as Wang and Commodore – which never quite made it to the Los Angeles of the future as envisaged by the filmmakers. You won't see Microsoft [established 1975] or Apple [1976].

FURTHER READINGS

The Risky Business of Diversification, Ralph Biggadike, Harvard Business Review, May 1979. Although Biggadike looked at large businesses, this classic article is still worth a read if you want a better understanding of the dangers of diversification. Even large corporations struggle, and in general, see many years of continuous investment before they reap a return.

In *Growth, Diversification, and Business Group Formation in Entrepreneurial Firms* [Small Business Economics 25, pages 65–82 (2005)], Iacobucci and Rosa discuss the way in which entrepreneurial firms manage diversification risk through setting up entities that are separate but under the founders' control.

Bottled for Business: The Less Gassy Guide to Entrepreneurship (1st Edition) Paperback, Karan Bilimoria, 2007, Capstone.

Hunters and Farmers: There's a useful elaboration of this concept and the roles played by each type in https://blog.close.com/hunter-farmer-sales/

2

CHALLENGE TO GROWTH NUMBER TWO: MONEY, MONEY, MONEY

INTRODUCTION

In a previous chapter, we discussed conversations with Business Growth Programme participants about their aspirations. This is a selection of what they typically tell us on entering the programme: "I want to build a £10 mn business." "I want to build a £20 mn business." Very occasionally, "I want to build a £100 mn business." When we ask what that target number represents, it's invariably the sales figure. What about profit or cash generation, we ask. Mostly these numbers take a back seat, respondents admit, although their importance is acknowledged. Sometimes this leads to a further question: "Would you rather run a business with a turnover of £10 mn, producing 5% net profit and leaking cash; or a business turning over £5 mn, producing 10% net profit and generating cash? Each is delivering £500,000 net." There usually follows a pause for thought.

If you're fluent in finance and accounting, you may want to skip the next few pages. Alternatively, you may see the value of taking a short refresher course. We say this because even BGP

DOI: 10.4324/9781003410614-3

participants who have an MBA or accounting qualification admit they tend to leave money matters to their book-keepers or accountants, and confess to losing sight of the bigger picture.

A large part of the finance and accounting function in any business is essentially technical: making sure that the correct figures are entered in the correct columns, for instance, or familiarity with the workings of commonly used accounting software. Rather, what we are concerned with in this chapter is twofold:

- clearing up some widely held misunderstandings about what financial reporting tells the business owner
- and directing your attention to what you really need to know to keep on top of your business's finances

It's still surprising to us how many otherwise gifted and skilled business founders lack even the rudiments of an understanding of how money works in their business. It's a little like being a pilot without really knowing how to interpret the instrumentation dials in the cockpit. If you just press on and trust to luck and the manufacturers, the plane will somehow make it across the Atlantic. That's not much comfort to the passengers – or the other aircrew – and, by analogy, the staff in the business. A plane might run on autopilot, but a growing business definitely won't.

A major revelation on the [Business Growth] Programme was that Rob learned to love numbers. "I had no interest before," he says. "If our finance department told me we had a million pounds in the bank, that was, oh, okay." Now Data Image has the reporting systems that enable him to understand exactly how and where the firm is making money, almost to the nearest penny. "Numbers tell a story," he says. "BGP taught me that, and now I can't get enough data!".
(Robert Farfort, Founder and CEO Data Image Group.
Taken from a presentation to BGP class, 2021)

There's another, more sinister reason why ambitious business founders who are not content with the status quo might want to brush up on their numeracy. Fraud. Expansion has its downside, in that the potential for misappropriation of funds grows with the business, as we shall see.

PROFIT AND CASH

Here's a question for you. The difference between net profit as stated in the accounts and cash on the balance sheet is explained by:

a) Non-cash factors, such as depreciation of assets and amortisation of goodwill or intellectual property
b) Non-cash factors as above, plus net cash – plus or minus – produced from any disposal and/or acquisition of fixed assets
c) Timing differences between making the sale and receiving the cash for that sale
d) b) and c) above, plus other adjustments to working capital
e) A smart accountant

Congratulations if you answered d). As it happens, there may actually be very little difference between a business's cash generation and its net profit, if the factors referred to in a), b), c) and d) are minimal. Many service businesses operate quite successfully with little in the way of fixed assets, have grown organically so have no need to amortise goodwill, have no IP to speak of, and no stock or any significant work in progress to adjust for: they sell time, lease their buildings and equipment, and their assets are basically the people they employ. The biggest discrepancy between reported profit and cash in the business is often the lag between invoicing their clients and being paid.

As we've already noted, businesses reporting a profit can still go bust. Businesses which run out of cash inevitably do.

BUSINESS MODELS THAT WORK

To explore this in greater depth, let's contrast and compare two types of business: the supermarket chain and the construction company.

Supermarket chains in most economies operate with long-term net profit margins of between 2% and 5%. This fact surprises many people and, considered in isolation, prompts the question, how do they stay in business? Most entrepreneurs would expect to see a bottom line percentage in their businesses at least twice as large.

The answer lies in part in the supermarkets' economies of scale and scope: big stores purchase in bulk, which ensures gross margins high enough to cover their extensive infrastructure costs of warehousing, transportation, local business taxes, freezers and chiller cabinets and so forth. But the major part of the reason for their success as a business model lies in *their capacity to generate huge amounts of cash*. Store customers pay at the cash till. Suppliers of the goods that fill the shelves are paid 45, 60 [or even more] days in arrears. If a popular line is being replenished several times a week, you can see that a multiplier effect is taking place: the supermarket is taking in an ever-growing amount of cash before it pays out. Before most everyday purchases became electronic, it was a common sight to see security guards emptying cash registers in stores once a day at the minimum. Supermarkets were swamped with hard cash.

A business can survive, indeed thrive, on low net margins if it generates cash in sufficient volumes. You could liken this type of business model to a cow that is constantly grazing.

The construction business serves as an example of a very different model, the project type. Excluding house-building for the private market, construction firms sell to business and government. They get paid in lump sums, typically at stage points defined by contract, and that relationship with the customer often endures over years until the job is completed. Businesses based on the project model cannot generate cash in the same way that a super-market does, because their cash receipts are "lumpy", while their outgoings, in the form of raw materials and labour, are frequent and recurrent. This kind of business is more like an anaconda, say, which consumes large prey at irregular intervals – but the food is enough to keep it going until the next opportunity.

Non-domestic construction is also a relatively low-margin industry: a successful player might consistently return an average net profit of 5%. The trick lies in the accurate estimation of project costs and ensuring that stage payments are suitably timed and large enough to make sure the business never runs out of working capital and remains in profit. The notorious UK construction firm Carillion referred to in the last chapter went bust for multiple reasons, but two major factors in its downfall were the unprofitability of the projects it secured through underbidding, and that its public sector customers were very slow payers. When the money did eventually come in, it was not enough. Carillion survived as long as it did only by stretching payment of its army of small subcontractors as far as it possibly could. Finally it ran, quite literally, out of road.

IT'S ALL ABOUT MARGINS

The point of the examples above is to show that it *is* possible to run a successful business on low net profit margins, but *only* if the cashflow works in your favour. It is, however, hard for many business founders to *grow* a business on low net margins. Without outside investment, relatively low retained earnings carried from one year to the next cumulate over time to a weaker balance sheet. That has implications for the business's credit rating – which may impact on how you are viewed by suppliers as well as buyers – as well as your capacity to borrow. It will certainly affect the valuation of the enterprise as and when the founder would like to exit. Above all, it is often the case that the margins in the business don't fully reflect *the value to the customer.*

FOOD FOR THOUGHT #5

Nick Jenkins is the founder of the company that revolutionised the personalised greetings cards market, Moonpig. In 1999 he saw the new possibilities afforded by the internet, and seized them. As well as designing its own cards, Moonpig struck deals with producers of greeting cards, enabling the business to offer a broad range of cards to customers, which they could personalise once they had made their choice of card. Moonpig took payment at the time of purchase, enabled the buyer to customise the greeting online, printed the card, and sent it in the post. For three years Nick priced his main product range at £1.99 per customised card. The cost of production was £0.99, which meant a gross margin of roughly 50%. Throughout that period the business ran at a loss, necessitating fresh injections of external funds. In 2002 Nick was finally persuaded by a fellow director that he was under-pricing the cards and that the customer would be perfectly willing to pay more. The price was increased to £2.99 per card, raising the gross margin to 66%, as there was no change to the cost of production. His fellow director was right. There was no impact on sales at all, but the company's cash position improved overnight!

Source: Moonpig case study

Received wisdom in manufacturing businesses is that a minimum gross margin of 40%[1] is needed for a company to be viable in the long term: anything less than 40% will be insufficient to cover the overhead costs of running the business and to deliver enough return to justify the investment *and* provide for putting money back in to replace or refurbish assets, buy raw materials and so forth. In the service sector, where the commodity being sold is essentially time, a widely used rule of thumb is that the direct cost of an employee's time needs to be marked up by 300% – i.e., by a factor of three – to create an adequate return.

Under-pricing of what they sell is surprisingly common among entrepreneurial businesses: on entry to the Business Growth Programme, we habitually challenge participants to raise their prices. Many are reluctant to do so. We have concluded there are two main reasons that explain this:

- *Historical legacy.* Many founders get into business in the first place by pricing their products or services cheaply. The thinking is that this makes purchase attractive, not just because the price is low, but because the lower the price, the lower the perceived risk on the part of the buyer. If an early customer of Moonpig's was unhappy with their purchase, they had only £1.99 to lose. Pricing low may make sense as a market entry strategy, but it rarely makes sense as a growth strategy. When BGP participants overcome their reservations and actually raise their prices, they typically find that the business makes more money overall and that any customers they lose tend to be unprofitable or awkward ones anyway! But it takes courage and nerve to make this step.
- *Founders frequently don't understand the value their business delivers from the customer's perspective.* In its early days, Moonpig customers were typically well-paid professionals who valued the convenience of the service, the choice of cards – especially the humorous ones – and the ability to customise and personalise the greeting. The price was not an issue. At £2.99, the purchase still seemed to represent good value for money. As we noted in the previous chapter, it appears to take a number of years of trading before a business founder really understands their marketplace.

Another factor may also be at play: what social psychologists define as loss aversion. If faced with a choice, many of us would prefer to stick with what we have – the known quantity – and not jeopardise this in pursuit of the bigger prize – the unknown quantity. However, this quite understandable instinct often defies numerical logic. The mathematical relationship between changes in gross margin [resulting from price rises or reductions], and the impact on sales volumes is widely misunderstood. It is not linear. Take a business with a gross margin of 40%. If it *increases* prices by an average of 2%, sales volume will have to fall by at least 5% before the gross margin drops. Conversely, if the same business *decreases* its average price by 2%, sales volumes will have to rise by 5% to compensate and restore the gross margin. In short:

- If you put up your prices, you can afford to lose a significant proportion of your customers [it all depends on your gross margin % as to how much business you can afford to lose and be no worse off]. In fact, you will reduce your working capital requirement by reducing turnover.
- If you reduce your selling price, and hence gross margin, you will have to win a disproportionate amount of new business to compensate for the lost gross margin.

You can see why BGP participants are challenged to raise their prices. At the end of this chapter, you will find a "ready reckoner" that shows the impact of price rises and decreases across a range of gross margins and sales volumes.

OVERDRAFT DEPENDENCE

Another factor that impacts business margins is likely to be the cost of finance. Many founders become over-reliant on – even addicted to – short-term finance as a means of funding the growth of their business. Most commonly this takes the form of overdraft finance or short-term loans, much loved by the banks since these are highly lucrative forms of lending. Raising money in a hurry is expensive. But it's not hard to see a mismatch between the business strategy and the financial strategy, if the one is focused on the long term and the other is preoccupied with the short term.

In 2010 Hotel Chocolat came up with a highly innovative means of financing its growth by issuing "chocolate bonds". A bond is essentially a promise to repay a certain sum within a defined period and carries an annual coupon, or rate of interest. Hotel Chocolat's offer was unusual and attracted much media attention. The vast majority of commercial bonds are issued by publicly traded companies and are usually targeted towards professional investors, who can then make a secondary market in the trading of bonds. Hotel Chocolat aimed its offer at its own customer base and instead of an interest payment its purchasers received chocolate in return. It was so successful a second bond issue was launched in 2014. Buyers of £2,000 bonds received six free Tasting Boxes per year, equivalent to a 5.38% return or 6.72% gross return for a basic rate taxpayer, while investors in the £4,000 bond received thirteen Tasting Boxes per year, equivalent to a 5.83% return or 7.29% gross return for a basic rate taxpayer.

The £6.4 mn raised was repaid roughly two years after the business was listed on the London Stock Exchange as Hotel Chocolat Group plc. In the words of the company, the chocolate bonds helped to create 600 jobs, open new stores and develop cocoa sustainability projects in St Lucia and Ghana.

FOOD FOR THOUGHT #6

Some thoughts on different approaches to funding a business:

FIRST, have you really looked at all the alternatives? Do you indeed know what all the alternatives are? When was the last time you went into the market place or took independent advice on your financial structure? Apart from all the mechanisms of debt finance such as factoring and invoice discounting, have you considered an injection of equity from an outside investor? The number of business angel investors and private equity houses has increased hugely in recent years. Many owner-managers view outside investment with great suspicion, but there is plenty of evidence that this brings greater stability to the business and relatively little loss of control.

SECOND, is the real reason why you are forced into expensive, short-term financing that you just aren't delivering adequate margins? It may well be that the business is not producing a large enough return to re-invest and fund its working capital. Are you charging enough? Do your customers fully understand the value they are receiving? Have you even told them? On the costs side, do you have the best terms from your suppliers? Could you get a better deal on office staples and utilities bills by joining a buying consortium, for example? Do you review your supplier base annually and set targets for improvement, or do you just accept the terms as given?

THIRD, is your working capital working as hard as it should do? Have you let your debtor days creep up, or do you keep these constantly under review? Is someone in the office tasked specifically with chasing late payers? Do you have a well-defined process for getting the money in? If your debtor days are currently sixty, you won't bring them down to thirty overnight. But with focus and dedicated effort, you could almost certainly reduce them to forty-five days within twelve to eighteen months – we know it's possible because we've seen literally dozens of owner-managed businesses achieve that sort of dramatic improvement.

Extracted from "From Brand Me to Brand Business: the bridge that every ambitious entrepreneur has to cross to create independent value" © David Molian

SQUEEZING CASH OUT OF THE BUSINESS

Of course very few businesses have the advantages of a well-known consumer brand and 100,000 loyal subscribers. There are simpler and quicker approaches to checking whether you can squeeze more money from your operating model, which may produce the cash to fuel your business's growth. The best place to start is usually by reviewing the credit control process within the business. Who, specifically, is responsible for getting the cash in? What precisely is their remit, what authority do they have, and what support might they require? Asking these questions might seem almost absurdly naïve, but unquestioned assumptions too often render a business unnecessarily fragile.

When Lan-tec took part in the Business Growth Programme in the late 2000s, it was a fast-growing supplier of ATMs [cash-withdrawal machines] and other financial transaction equipment. In the year prior to attending, turnover was £16 mn and net profit 3%. In the year following attendance, turnover was £15 mn and net profit 7%. When we visited the business, we were curious to know more about this transformation in performance. The directors told us that, among other things, the company's financing costs had reduced dramatically. By a relentless focus on their cashflow, the business had renegotiated payment terms with major customers, so that from being paid for 60 days in arrears, installations were now paid for upfront. How did you do it, we asked. It was a combination of factors:

- shining a spotlight on this part of the business and setting improvement targets, so that credit control staff knew exactly what was expected of them
- having greater confidence in themselves, i.e., mustering the courage to start potentially difficult conversations
- demonstrating the added value contributed by Lan-tec *from the customer's perspective*
- ceasing to do business with late payers
- and losing unprofitable business

Chasing customers for payment is not something that comes naturally to many people. It raises the spectre of awkward or uncomfortable conversations and, unsurprisingly, employees will often postpone the day or approach it obliquely – by repeatedly sending statements of overdue accounts, for instance – rather than pick up the phone. Lara Morgan [BGP 1999], founder of Pacific Direct and entrepreneur extraordinaire, introduced a novel way to resolve this reluctance among her own employees to take on the task. She invented a credit control chief, Mrs x, who was in charge of getting the money in from slow payers. Mrs x was a tough cookie, who sent uncompromising correspondence by post and email demanding payment and refusing to take no for an answer. On the rare occasions cowering customers picked up the phone and asked to speak to Mrs x, she was always out of the office; her colleagues, however, were happy to take her calls and accept payment on her behalf, while agreeing with the caller that Mrs x was indeed a hard nut.

LATERAL THINKING

When we review a company's financial performance over a time period, we are typically presented with a sheet of figures, laid out portrait-style, which we scan from top to bottom. Let's take the monthly management profit and loss accounts. At the top are the sales numbers and at the bottom are the net profits [or losses]. In between we see direct and indirect costs, specified by whatever level of reporting detail is thought necessary to understand how the business is performing. If there are multiple product/service lines we could see several sales lines showing the revenue earned per line and, if we require it, some supplementary analysis of the direct costs of each, so that we know the gross margin broken down by product type. A simple example is shown in Figure 2.1.

From such reports, we can track a number of indicators over time. These show us how well the business is performing, the aim being to reinforce success and take early action to correct problems. The metrics are money and percentages.

Simplified trading accounts P&L [Income] Statement

Item	£000	%	Metric
Net Sales	1000		
Direct cost of sales	500	50	Gross margin
Marketing	50		
Administration	250		
Directors salaries	100		
Other overheads	50		
Total Indirects	450	45	Indirects as % of sales
Net before tax	50	5	Net trading margin

Figure 2.1   Standardised Trading Reporting Statement.

Nothing new about this you might say, and you'd be right. This is **a** standard representation of how numerous business owners review and manage their firms, month in, month out. However, there is another way of looking at how the business is doing, and that is a lateral perspective, showing the two key processes for managing money, and specifically the cash position: **from invoice to cash** and **from purchase to payment** (see Figure 2.2).

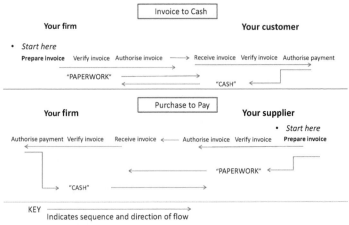

Figure 2.2   Simplified Financial Process Flows Across the Business.

In accordance with established practice, we use terms like "cash" and "paperwork" when in the modern age both communications and payments are almost exclusively electronic, but you get the picture. We also measure these processes primarily by time, in units of days.

FROM INVOICE TO CASH

To state the obvious, invoicing a customer is what triggers payment and the aim is to get the cash due into the business as quickly as possible and in full. [This is subject to modification in your terms of trade, such as a discount for prompt payment or a surcharge for late payment.] Your business generates the paperwork and the customer sends you money. Figure 2.2 shows in simplified form the basic processes:

- the information required to prepare the invoice that is being pulled together
- the draft invoice undergoing some form of verification and authorisation, typically against a purchase order
- a final invoice being prepared and sent to the customer

In a large and complex business, there may be numerous stages involved, but the invoicing process boils down to the same three basic things: preparation, checking/sign-off, and sending. In the early days much of this work – perhaps all of it – is done by one person, not infrequently the business founder. The tools to manage this are often improvised and stand apart from each other: the Excel spreadsheet is a trusty workhorse. But there comes a time in the life of a growing business when "good enough" is no longer good enough because the systems that served the business well in its infancy are no longer adequate. The most common symptoms that the business is under stress are:

- delays in preparing, verifying or authorising invoices, measured by time

- payment delays by customers [also measured by time], not necessarily because the customer is wilfully withholding payment but because the invoice does not comply with the customer's stipulations. It is important to grasp how many large firms *start* the process of paying suppliers. They pay only after they have received a statement, not on receipt of the invoice. That fact may well be buried in their Terms and Conditions.

Such changes in these metrics are early indicators of problems that need addressing.

When the cash is received by your firm, there will also be some process of reconciliation, to check that the cash received matches the invoice and, if not, that there is a good reason for this. And the cash received is also allocated to a specific customer account. This is essentially basic book-keeping and is within the remit of your external auditors to check. If your business is fortunate enough to be paid in advance, such as in the case of Lan-tec described above, or sells direct to consumers, the process of getting the money in is greatly simplified.

FROM PURCHASE TO PAYMENT

In the purchase-to-payment sequence of transactions, the roles of customer and supplier are reversed, and the processes are a mirror image [again, see Figure 2.2]. In exchange for the correct paperwork following receipt of goods and services, your supplier gets cash. Again, *as a customer*, you should only pay a supplier on receipt of a statement that you have reconciled internally.

CASHFLOW PROBLEMS?

Many business owners tell us that their first response to cash-flow problems is to delay payments to suppliers. Leaving aside the moral questions raised by the practice, this may work as a short-term expedient, but it is likely to have longer-term consequences. First, there is the reputational risk to your business. Suppliers can talk to each other and if you become known as a deliberately slow or reluctant payer, others are unlikely to do business with you except on hard-line terms. Second, and arguably more significantly, viewing additional "creditor strain" [as accountants put it] as the solution usually stops business owners from examining and correcting inefficiencies in the business. As we've outlined above, there are often easier and better ways to address the underlying problems.

GROWING BUSINESSES AND VULNERABILITIES

By definition, running a business involves financial transactions, and it's in the interests of every business owner to mitigate or eliminate the risks of moving money in and out of the business. Growing businesses, and especially those that are growing fast, are at greater risk because growth almost always comes with increased complexity. The founder can no longer hold the business in the palm of their hand, so to speak – and that renders the enterprise vulnerable. The co-founder of the Business Growth Programme, Colin Barrow, had a perfect description for this syndrome: too many businesses get bigger, but they don't grow up. If, as a parent, you addressed the needs of a growing child simply by buying new clothes, you'd end up with a case of arrested development. By analogy, a business that grows bigger but changes in no other respects is unlikely to enjoy a healthy maturity.

That vulnerability to financial loss or deterioration comes from both within and outside the company. We've talked above about the routine "good housekeeping" that the founder can undertake to tighten operations by looking across the basic processes. Good housekeeping is a constant process; but bigger interventions are required when there's a step-change in how the business operates.

LOSS OF CONTROL

It is frightening how quickly a fast-growing business can spiral out of control. The example that follows is drawn from the experience of the author. Some years ago I was involved with a consumer electronics business. The founder had spotted a new opportunity in the UK market and began trading by sourcing products from wholesalers in mainland Europe. Products were then sold online direct to individuals and small business owners at a healthy margin. This operating model continued for a couple of years. The upside was that very little stock was held in the company's warehouse, meaning that only a small amount of cash was tied up in working capital. The downside was that wholesalers took a fair slice of the value chain, reducing potential profits.

More players entered the British market and the sector grew rapidly. The founder decided that he would source most products direct from the Far East manufacturers, as he could now meet their minimum order requirements. This would be more profitable – at least on paper – and allow the business to expand its product range. The salesforce were suitably enthusiastic, excited by the opportunity to earn more money by selling more products. The founder was a highly persuasive individual who assured the board that the business could accommodate the change. Once it took place, the impact was visible in higher levels of stock filling the shelves in the firm's small warehouse, a greater number of individual stock items and a very different schedule of inward product deliveries. Shipments to customers also increased as the sales machine cranked up.

Within months it became clear that all was not well. Customers continued to pay cash with orders, but problems began to emerge. Instead of making money, the business was losing money. Sales were up, but profitability was down. More worryingly, the quantity and value of stock in the warehouse could not be reconciled with what was shown in the weekly reports. The frequency of stock-takes was increased, but the discrepancies continued. The atmosphere in the business grew increasingly tense and suspicious. Could the staff be stealing? Locks were changed and security cameras installed. It made no difference. Could there be accounting mistakes, or even fraud?

At considerable expense, a forensic accountant who specialised in detecting financial malpractice, was called in. He trawled through the book-keeping and reporting systems exhaustively. After several weeks he could find nothing wrong. Finally, an alternative explanation suggested itself to the board. Was the data generated by the systems the business relied on actually dependable? To keep costs down, it transpired that the founder at start-up had commissioned a bespoke IT system to manage the business processes, rather than buy a more expensive package off the shelf. The designer of the system was called in and presented with the state of affairs. He explained that the computer systems underpinning the business had been designed primarily to drive sales, not to manage stock. The systems worked fine when the sales volumes were low, the range of items sold was small, and the products requested were in stock – essentially the original trading business.

Further investigation revealed that on the rare occasions that a product was not in stock, the staff had got used to working **around** the system, keeping manual records of when an order was only part-filled or unfulfilled and adjusting the information on the system accordingly. When previously unavailable stock did arrive, it was relatively easy to check the records, call the customer, dispatch the item and generate another invoice.

On a small scale such manual "tweaking" had no real impact on operations. Under the emergent business model of a bigger product range and an altered pattern of deliveries, it caused problems that only multiplied with growing sales. The more you sold, the bigger the scope for confusion. The improvised workarounds could not keep pace and the IT systems were not sophisticated enough to deal with real-time out-of-stocks, part-fulfilment and back orders. Perhaps most crucially, the stock management system [such as it was] did not fully update the accounting systems in real time. In short, the business was out of control and could not be salvaged.

FRAUD

The events described took place a long time ago. Since then, affordable enterprise resource management [ERM] systems for smaller businesses, in many cases cloud-based, have become widely available. IT is today a relatively mature industry. A far greater current risk to a business's finances is likely to be posed by fraud.

The 2021 Fraud Report produced by money.co.uk posted that UK citizens suffered losses of £2.4 bn, with nearly half a million **reported** cases. That number was nearly twice the size of the previous year's. Cheque, card and online bank account fraud accounted for losses of £204 mn, computer service software £23.6 mn, and computer virus/malware/spyware: £1.2 mn.

The Report does not break down the losses suffered by individuals versus businesses, and does not speculate on how much fraud goes unreported. By definition, it is impossible to know how much fraud goes unreported, but there are good reasons to think that it is a lot, and that this reported figure of £2.4 bn is a gross underestimate of actual fraudulent activity in the economy as a whole. Take the third category referred to, computer virus/malware/spyware. According to the Fraud Report, just over 7,000 incidents were reported, which the Report concludes is an average cost per episode of £168 [£1.2 mn divided by roughly 7,000]. Private individuals might suffer a typical loss of that size, but the losses to business are likely to be several magnitudes greater.

A BGP participant recently reported that his company had been subject to a very sophisticated invoicing fraud of £100,000 which, after the involvement of his firm's lawyers, the bank agreed to refund – and his story is just one of many we have come across. In some cases, business owners have declined to report such fraud to the authorities themselves, leaving it to the banks to do so, citing their reasons variously as:

- a diversion from running the business
- a lack of confidence in the willingness of the police to investigate and prosecute
- preferring to keep the knowledge of this within the firm
- a belief that their time is better spent in strengthening their business's defences against future scams

It is beyond the scope of this book to give advice on the best technology strategies to improve your firm's security against cyber attack. That is better left to the technical experts in your company or within your bank. However, it is worth stating that this is unquestionably a war in which the criminals are becoming more ingenious every year and businesses that do not take cyber-security seriously put themselves at risk.

THE ENEMY WITHIN

It is a sad fact, but most episodes of fraud we have encountered within fast-growth businesses have occurred *inside* those companies, and in nearly every instance originate from the finance and accounting departments.

FOOD FOR THOUGHT #7

Patisserie Valerie began life in Soho in 1926, as an upscale vendor of patisseries, cakes and savouries. Initially, there was a single shop in Dean Street, London, W1. When the business was acquired from the founding family in 1987, a small expansion took place resulting in an additional eight branches, all in London's West End. In 2006, Risk Capital Partners acquired a controlling stake in the company, with a view to taking the business a stage further. Risk Capital's chairman, Luke Johnson, stated at the time:

> *We have significant experience of rolling out successful food and drink concepts, including Pizza Express, Strada and Giraffe. Patisserie Valerie is a much-loved institution with tremendous heritage. We are confident there are many upscale locations across Britain's cities that would love the authentic pastries, cakes and savouries supplied by Patisserie Valerie.*

A parent company, Patisserie Holdings, was created to facilitate the expansion of the brand. Johnson had good grounds for his confidence. In the 1990s Johnson and his then business partner Hugh Osmond had taken Pizza Express from 12 company-owned restaurants to over 250 and increased its share price from 40 pence to over £9. Johnson was regarded as one of the UK's leading and most successful entrepreneurs. A number of other brands were acquired by Patisserie Holdings and in 2014 the business was listed on AIM, London's junior stock market, as a public company, raising further cash for growth.

On 10 October 2018, the company's shares were suspended from trading. The company announced that the board had been notified of significant and potentially fraudulent accounting irregularities, that a potential material mis-statement of the company's accounts had significantly impacted the company's cash position, and that Chris Marsh, the chief financial officer, had been suspended from his role. Prior to suspension, the business had a market capitalisation of over £500 million. Despite an injection from Johnson of £20 mn, within three months Patisserie Holdings had collapsed into administration and the Fraud Squad was investigating unauthorised overdrafts. According to a statement issued by the company, the collapse was "a direct result of the significant fraud". Following an investigation by the Financial

> Reporting Council, the company's auditors were fined
> £2.3 mn because they had failed both to spot "red flags"
> and to question information provided by management.
>
> Source: assorted press reports

The point here is a simple one. If even an experienced mover and shaker like Luke Johnson [he was also Chairman of Channel Four Television from 2004 to 2010] can fall victim to fraud, it can happen to anyone. Admittedly this was a large and comparatively complex business, but Patisserie Holdings is a macro example of what many other businesses experience on a microscale. In this case, it seems to have been concealed overdrafts. Other sources of internal fraud reported by Business Growth Programme attendees include:

- bogus invoices submitted by phantom suppliers, usually created by someone with the sole authority to authorise payment: such instances can go undiscovered for years.
- unauthorised leasing arrangements, typically for company cars: one BGP participant sacked his finance director when he discovered that two illicit vehicle leases were in place, one for the use of the FD's spouse and the other for the couple's eldest child. The fraud was only discovered by chance when the firm's founder was having his own leased car serviced at the dealership used by his firm!
- payments due to creditors such as HMRC which have been diverted into personal bank accounts: such fraud is normally revealed by a final demand from the exasperated creditor.

ACCELERANTS

As discussed above, you need to establish a process of "good housekeeping" at regular intervals. It means taking a deep dive into your business's processes, which flow laterally across the firm. This could be likened to stapling yourself to an invoice, both outgoing and incoming, and walking a transaction through from start to finish. Remember the two words, *show me*. If you are dissatisfied with what you are being told, keep digging. If your gut tells you that something is not working as well as it should be, or is just plain wrong, trust your gut. You can always bring in expert assistance to support or allay your suspicions with hard evidence.

Ensure you are "easy to do business with". It's simple to add unnecessary complexity to a business's operations. Every so often, you should expect to weed out processes that impede the ability of the business to serve its customers and receive prompt payment in return.

No one in the business marks their own homework. From the finance director downwards, no one involved in handling money should be allowed to do so in isolation. Fraud flourishes when checks and controls are inadequate.

Upgrade your advisers. You need advice that is appropriate for the business you aspire to become, not necessarily for the business as it currently is. Many founders start by using the services of the small local accountancy firm and continue to do so long after their firms have outgrown the capability of that adviser to provide the required expertise. Karan Bilimoria engaged a mid-tier firm of auditors from the early days of Cobra Beer, viewing this not so much as a cost but as an investment in Cobra's future. The fees incurred cost more than was strictly necessary but provided the business with the skills and networks to support the founder's vision for the future.

BEARTRAPS AND BLOCKERS

Never, ever, run out of cash. It is good practice to work on a three-month or thirteen-week rolling cashflow forecast: a window that captures reliable and credible working assumptions, allowing enough time in which to foresee problems and take corrective action.

Work through the implications of a step-change in the business model in advance of implementation. By nature, most business founders are impatient and driven by new opportunities. But new opportunities frequently bring with them changes and challenges to the way the business works. One significant change, for instance to the supplier base, can flow through to other parts of how the business works, as we've seen above.

Do not assume that the function of external accounts preparation or auditing is to spot fraud. In the light of recent episodes like Patisserie Holdings, pressure has been put on the accountancy profession to tighten up its supervision and avoid conflicts of interest. That said, fraud is often notoriously hard to detect. It is far better to install the right checks and controls as preventative measures, which is certainly something that an expert can advise on.

SUMMARY

In this second chapter, we have invited you to examine whether your business's finances are in the best possible shape to support growth. Very few business founders are financial experts, but there are certain key aspects of how money works in a business which are important for the boss to grasp. Through an improved understanding of these, ambitious founders raise their chances of enhancing their firms' performance, and protecting their businesses from avoidable risks:

- Profit and cash in a company are not the same thing. Businesses go bust not necessarily because they are unprofitable, but because they run out of money.
- It is possible to run a successful business on low net profit margins, but only if the cashflow works in your favour. It is, however, hard for many business founders to *grow* a business on low net margins.

- Make sure you understand the value you deliver from the customer's perspective, and charge accordingly.
- Reliance on short-term funding is out of sync with long-term ambitions, and too frequently hides inefficiencies within the business.
- Look for ways to squeeze more cash from your working capital by first understanding and then improving the way cash flows across your business.
- Understand the full implications of changes to your supply chains and buying patterns *before* you introduce these.
- Your internal auditors will advise you on introducing the checks and controls that minimise the possibility of internal fraud, but do not expect external auditors to spot fraud as part of their routine work. Every so often, take a deep dive into your business's systems and be prepared to challenge anything that looks out of the ordinary.
- Consider upgrading your advisers – specifically accountants and law firms – to match the firm you aspire to become, not the firm you currently are.

	Existing % Gross Margin								
	5%	10%	15%	20%	25%	30%	35%	40%	50%
	% volume increase required to maintain gross								
%Price Reduction	margin								
2	67	25	15	11	9	7	6	5	4
3	150	43	25	18	14	11	9	8	6
4	400	67	36	25	19	15	13	11	9
5		100	50	33	25	20	17	14	11
7.5		300	100	60	43	33	27	23	18
10			200	100	67	50	40	33	25
15				300	150	100	75	60	43

	Existing % Gross Margin								
	5%	10%	15%	20%	25%	30%	35%	40%	50%
	% volume decrease required to maintain gross								
%Price Increase	margin								
2	29	17	12	9	7	6	5	5	4
3	37	23	17	13	11	9	8	7	6
4	44	29	21	17	14	12	10	9	7
5	50	33	25	20	17	14	12	11	9
7.5	60	43	33	27	23	20	18	16	13
10	67	50	40	33	29	25	22	20	17
15	75	60	50	43	37	33	30	27	23

Figure 2.3 Volume-margin-price Changes Ready Reckoner.

NOTE

1 This rule of thumb generally applies to smaller manufacturing businesses: in larger businesses, gross margins in successful firms can vary more widely across sectors.

FURTHER READINGS

The 2021 Fraud Report www.money.co.uk

The Secrets of the Seven Alchemists, John Rosling, Harriman House, 2014.

The Genghis Khan Guide to Business by Brian Warnes is invaluable. Although long out of print, copies can be obtained from Amazon: www.amazon.co.uk/Genghis-Guide-Business-Charles-Warnes/dp/0950943207

The Bottom Line: Business Finance: Your Questions Answered, Paul Barrow, Virgin Books, 2005. Available at: www.amazon.co.uk/Bottom-Line-Business-Questions-Answered/dp/0753509989. In 2024, this should also be available in a revised version as an eBook.

Ex-BGPer and forensic financial specialist Peter Charles features some excellent videos on his firm's website, which take a close look at a variety of finance topics. See www.petercharles.co.uk.

On combatting cyber attacks and pre-empting these by building resilience, see https://lnkd.in/eeQAsRkH.

3

CHALLENGE TO GROWTH NUMBER THREE: MANAGERIAL STYLES
OR WHY SUPER-HEROES NEED NOT APPLY

INTRODUCTION

Cast your mind back to the early days when you started the business. To get the company up and running, how many of the basic tasks did you – or your co-founders – take on yourself? Who found premises in which to start the firm? Who set up your banking arrangements? Who was the chief salesperson? Who sent the invoices? Who sorted out the IT? Who maintained the books and dealt with the bank, the accountants and the law firm? Who was responsible for hiring new staff and firing under-performers?

If you are like nearly every business founder we have met, the answer is you/your business partner[s]. At start-up and early-stage, the entrepreneur is invariably chief cook and bottle-washer. There's seldom enough cash or sufficient hours in the day to deal with everything that needs doing. You start early and finish late. To anyone who is looking to start a business, we strongly recommend an iron constitution and a ferocious work ethic.

For businesses that aspire to grow successfully, this state of affairs cannot persist indefinitely. At some point, the founder has to do less of the doing and more of the planning. As the

DOI: 10.4324/9781003410614-4

co-founder of the Business Growth Programme, Colin Barrow, [citing the great Peter Drucker] argued, a leader has three essential tasks:

- to run today's business
- to make today's business better
- and to create a new business for tomorrow

At the crux of this is how a business founder chooses to spend their time. In this chapter we explore the challenge of how founders can make that transition from being consumed by running today's business to improving it and, ultimately, refashioning it for the demands of tomorrow. This marks the third leg in our analysis of how to get your current business in the best possible shape for growth – and how you can change your role, if required, to achieve your personal ambitions.

FOOD FOR THOUGHT #8

Every ambitious entrepreneur has their sights set on creating a business with independent value. Admittedly, not everyone starts a business with a view to selling it. Some people will want to hand the business over to the next generation of their family. Others are just in love with what they do and plan to keep growing and developing their businesses as long as their health allows them to. But a true test of the maturity of any independently owned and managed firm is whether you are working for the business, or whether the business is working for you. Only when you can honestly say that the business is working for you do you have a business that has independent value.

We're not just playing with words here. One of the commonest complaints we hear from owner-managers is that too much of the time it seems as if the business is running them, and not vice versa. Their days are spent fighting fires, solving problems brought to them by other people, checking that staff are doing their jobs properly, soothing irate customers, negotiating with suppliers: the list is endless. They *know* they should be spending more time improving today's business and shaping the business for the future, but somehow the good intentions are always on the back burner.

Brand Me

If this sounds like you, don't worry. You are definitely not alone. I would guess that this is how many owner-managers feel, quite possibly most of the time. The shared problem is that they are stuck in the zone that is *Brand Me*. In the Brand Me zone, the business is in all essentials an extension of the founder and owner-manager. The business has no real existence independently of the boss – or bosses, in the case of partnerships. Of course, if the firm is a limited company or partnership, *legally* the business is a separate entity. But the reality is that *commercially* the business is little more than an appendage of the owner(s). And when the boss is away for any length of time, the business starts to languish, just like an organ which is cut off from the blood supply. Why else do so many owner-managers take so little holiday? And when they do, why do they spend so much time checking their emails, reading text messages and calling the office?

Brand Business

The converse of Brand Me is *Brand Business*. In the Brand Business zone, the business is genuinely separable from the owner-manager. He or she can take time away from the business, without the constant need to phone in or experiencing a low-level, nagging anxiety, always in the background. In this zone the staff know what needs to be done, and do it. They deal with the routine, every-day decisions and only refer issues by exception. People know where the business is going, and they understand the part that they play in making this happen. The main value added by the boss is in setting the strategic direction and enabling the employees to perform to the best of their abilities. And the biggest pay-off is that in the Brand Business zone the business is much, much more likely to have value as an entity independently of the owner.

Shangri-La or the Promised Land?

It might sound like we're relocating to Fantasy Island, but Brand Business is a reality for a select number of owner-managers whom we talk to every day. More to the point, programmes like the Business Growth and Development Programme (BGP) have helped hundreds of owner-managers actively cross the bridge. Before we examine how an owner-manager makes the transition from one zone to the other, take a minute to answer our ten-question test, to discover where you and your business are currently located:

Which Zone Are You In?

1. Are you the chief sales person?
2. Are you the major point of contact for key customers?
3. Are you the major point of contact for key suppliers?
4. Do you personally negotiate all contracts of significance?
5. Are you supporting the business with personal bank guarantees?

6. Do you routinely answer day-to-day queries from staff?
7. Are you working in excess of 40 hours a week in the business?
8. Are you the chief – and frequently the only – firefighter?
9. Do you spend fewer than five hours a week planning and discussing the future of the business?
10. Do you lack any colleagues in the business with whom you can discuss your hopes and fears openly and honestly?

For every Yes, score yourself one point.

If your score is:

3 *or under*: Congratulations! You've completed the transition to *Brand Business*, or are well on the way to doing so.

3–6: *Well done.* You're on the right track. Keep going!

7 *or over*: You're still firmly on the *Brand Me* side of the bridge.

Everyone starts as Brand Me

Every start-up is a Brand Me business. In the early days the founder is asking investors, customers, suppliers and new recruits to take a leap of faith and place their trust in him or her. No matter how clever or compelling the idea, or patentable the technology, all these supporters of a new venture are ultimately betting on the vision, courage and stamina of the business founder. That's just as true of a business concept which is built around a strong branded proposition from the word go, as it is of any other type of start-up.

Extracted from *From Brand Me to Brand Business* © David Molian

MAPPING THE BUSINESS FOUNDER'S JOURNEY

In 1988 the Business Growth Programme was created to satisfy a need unrecognised by most business schools. Entrepreneurship was just at the point of being taken seriously as a career alternative to joining a big company or working in the professions. Governments and policy-makers had begun to understand that creating and growing new businesses was the best means of stimulating growth and revitalising national economies. Business schools, on the other hand, were largely preoccupied with their historic role as training grounds for entry into large corporations, banks and management consultancies. The scant management education for small businesses which existed at that time was on the whole undifferentiated, designed to teach small business owners how to become better at running their small businesses. Yet it was clear that an emerging breed of ambitious business founders aspired to transform what were essentially large small companies into small big companies. To help them realise their goals, they would need something different from the mainstream management development then on offer.

Designing a programme for this audience was in itself an entrepreneurial venture. For one thing, the creators had to overcome no small amount of institutional inertia and scepticism. But, once a successful prototype was launched and the concept was proven, a better understanding of the needs of participants steadily grew. It became clear that the existing, well-publicised academic models that described and predicted the growth of entrepreneurial businesses had certain limitations. These tended to take a similar form: stage models[1] which predicted different phases of development and managerial style, in line with the firm's growth in revenue and headcount. The phases the models described were essentially linear and sequential; it was assumed that a constantly growing business would progress from one phase to the next and, in the case of the Greiner model, encounter foreseeable crises which would trigger the next stage of development, providing the founder/owner could weather the storm.

In the classroom, however, as BGP participants told their stories, matters were not so clear-cut. Even though the theory behind these models was based on research in the field, the growth journeys they depicted often failed to match the lived experience of business founders. First, many participants described the history of their businesses as not linear, but more like a game of snakes and ladders. For a couple of years, say, the business made good progress [going up the ladder] and then met with obstacles that formed a brick wall and sent it back down the snake, reversing all the forward momentum. Sometimes events beyond the control of the business, such as dramatic changes in the marketplace, were obvious factors in the setbacks. More often than not, however, the founders we met believed that they were doing the right things in a benign environment, but something was preventing them from breaking through.

Second, and related to the first point, the models were long on description but short on guidance. Even if a stage model corresponded to a participant's experience, it offered limited practical advice on how a business founder needed to modify their managerial behaviour, to steer the business successfully from one stage of development to the next.

A better understanding of that journey was required.

THE ARTISAN-HERO-MEDDLER-STRATEGIST MODEL

Through intensive conversations with business owners aspiring to grow, a new model was designed, with the aim of enhancing founders' understanding of their own past and current behaviour, and how that matched – or mismatched – the needs of the business if it was to develop and mature. By means of a diagnostic survey, this model benchmarked the key skills required to grow the business against the way in which the founder/owner/boss spent his or her time. The axes of the model are shown in Figure 3.1:

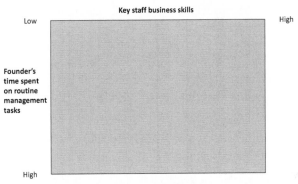

Figure 3.1   Skills Required Versus Founder's Time.
Source: the author

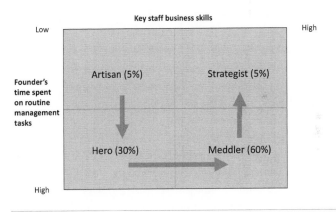

Key: arrows indicate typical progression over time

Figure 3.2   Skills Required Versus Founder's Time: Analysis by Quadrant.
Source: the author

This model was further developed into a matrix of four quadrants, each depicting a distinct managerial style, or type, the purpose being to illustrate the founder's journey and to enable BGP participants to identify their own predominant stage of development (Figure 3.2).

The basis of the model was to lay out the changes in managerial behaviour required for the business to grow and develop over time, in accordance with the tasks formulated by Drucker described above. The figures in brackets represent the dominant mode of behaviour which those who complete the survey typically identified with prior to the start of the Business Growth Programme.

THE ARTISAN MODE

Virtually every business begins life as an "artisan" business. That is to say, the founder and the initial team which he or she has assembled are heavily, if not exclusively, focused on selling the product of their professional skill or service: plumbers do plumbing, software developers write code, web designers design websites, law firms provide legal services, recruitment consultancies hunt for clients and candidates, and so on. Nearly all the time is spent on the "doing", since the business will only survive if it is able to attract and retain customers. In these very early days the business normally requires only the basic management skills of book-keeping, processing sales, securing the necessary office supplies, maintaining the minimum IT systems, replying to enquiries, and so on. While in this mode, the enterprise looks very similar to any other small business, and the founder's time is spent doing pretty much what any small business owner is doing. Time spent away from the actual "doing" is time not devoted to earning the money needed for the firm's survival, so routine management is kept to a minimum. In other words, it is in the founder's interests to keep the overheads as low as possible and so a large part of the daily maintenance needed to keep the business going is undertaken by the founder. The aim of the first year of operations is, after all, to survive to the end of the first year of operations.

This phase of the business's life is normally a short one, if the founder has ambitions to grow – which is why only a very small proportion of entrants to BGP – around 5% – identify themselves as predominantly artisans.[2]

THE HERO MODE

As the enterprise survives and grows, the burden of routine management can only increase. More business activity requires more administration, some of which can be automated but some, inevitably, requires human intervention. Gradually the role of the founder begins to change. As you can see in the quadrant analysis in Figure 3.2, the demands on the founder for dealing with daily tasks tend to mount. The business is still at a stage where it cannot support much overhead and the founder is understandably reluctant to pay the large salaries needed to attract well-qualified staff in areas such as Finance, Marketing and IT systems. The corollary of this is that the routine decisions which would otherwise be taken by those able to make the call will be referred to the founder. He or she typically finds themselves at the end of a growing barrage of questions from staff. For instance, customer A wants product x, but it is not in stock. Product x can be obtained at short notice from a stockist we don't normally use, but at a higher price. Customer A is a valued customer. Do we meet their order and take the hit on margin, or should we pass the extra cost to the customer? Customer B is a late payer. Their credit rating is in decline. Should we continue to supply them, or put a stop on their credit until the overdue account is settled? Customer C wants us to supply an overseas subsidiary. Which currency should we invoice them in, and should the price be increased to reflect the additional costs incurred in export?

This is just a sample of the kind of daily decisions that face the approximately 30% of BGP founders who identify themselves as being predominantly in the hero phase of their journey. The role has been likened to that of a performing seal [an act which thankfully has largely disappeared]: the better the seal is at doing the trick, the more fish get thrown at it so it can repeat the trick or perform the next one. The more decisions the founder makes, the more they are likely to be presented with. The underlying problem is twofold: employees are not empowered to make these kinds of decisions [quite possibly for good reasons], and there are no systems in place to manage routine decision-making and to refer only the exceptions.

Being a hero is gratifying to the ego and also addictive. It satisfies a basic human need, and many "heroes" will tell you that after a day of solving other people's problems they feel not only good about themselves but have a sense of accomplishment. All of which may be true, but time spent in mundane problem-solving is time not spent improving today's business or preparing it for tomorrow – it's a brake on growth.

THE MEDDLER MODE

As time goes on the volume of demands made on the boss to determine such decisions typically becomes unsustainable. Things can't continue like this, and the business owner/manager will begin the search to hire new people with the skills and experience to make his or her life tolerable again. Recruitment typically starts at the point of greatest pain, such as managing Sales and Marketing, or Financial Control. Finding the right key staff is often a challenge in its own right, since the people you'd most like to attract are either too expensive or would prefer to work for a more established business which can offer a better package of benefits as well as higher pay. However, you persist and eventually you fill the vacancy. In some instances, if the business can afford it or the circumstances are dire enough, you might hire for several key positions and an embryonic senior management team starts to take shape.

This is a big leap in a business's development. For one thing, recruitment carries with it a certain element of risk, even if it is done through a third party such as an agency. The job of the agency is to present you, the client, with a suitable shortlist of candidates, but it is down to the client to make the final selection. Very few of us are experts in hiring talent, and often we will go with our gut feel. Is the person likeable? Apart from their qualifications, will this person fit in with the culture of the company? Will he or she make a good colleague and adapt quickly to our sort of firm? We have yet to meet a business founder who, when the subject of recruitment comes up, does not admit to regrets.

It can help if someone from outside the business is invited to join an interviewing panel and give an objective view, but even this is not infallible. Some years ago, the author was asked to do just that by a very successful BGP business, which had decided to create the new post of Supply Chain Director. It was a big step, involving considerable internal reorganisation, and the business took the process seriously. After a day of meeting key members of the company, and another of actually touring operations, the preferred candidate was interviewed exhaustively by the panel. Everyone's opinions were then collated, and the unanimous verdict was that she be hired.

Within three months she had left. One of the main reasons for her interest in the job, she had said, was the opportunity to move into a fast-moving, entrepreneurial environment. Her CV certainly qualified her in terms of skills and experience. It also detailed her previous employment in large public companies. When confronted with the daily realities of a fast-moving entrepreneurial business and the absence of a large team and big company support, our appointee realised that she'd been entertaining a fantasy. Perhaps we should have probed her motivations more deeply and been more explicit about what life in the hiring business was like. Would it have made any difference? Many founders we know have experienced the same problem, and it creates a dilemma: you want the skills and experience of people who have worked in larger businesses, but you expect them to understand the smaller-business environment.

Regardless of how a business founder recruits new staff, an even bigger risk is in play: a failure on the part of the founder to realise that bringing in this first wave of new people changes the dynamics of the business – which in turn affects how the founder spends their time. The person who best knows how things are done in the business is, in the opinion of nearly all founders, the person who started the firm from scratch. The temptation, then, to interfere in other people's jobs is for some founders overwhelming. By far the largest proportion of entrants to BGP – around 60% – will identify themselves as predominantly meddlers. Even after new hires have been trained and inducted into the firm and are settled into their roles, the boss cannot hold back from telling them how to do their jobs. It's a particularly acute problem in many family businesses, where the current generation in charge is resistant to ceding authority to the incoming generation.

You will have noticed that we use the word *predominantly* a lot. This is because the self-diagnostic survey reveals that there are relatively few "pure" types of owner-manager behaviour: people whose managerial habits correspond solely to one mode of acting. This is particularly so in the case of the hero–meddler quadrants, where there is a marked overlap between the two. The same individual will exhibit the characteristics of both types, for which there is a prime explanation: many owner-managers swing between the two modes of behaviour. The reason seems to be that excessive meddling in other people's work tends to result in one of two outcomes. Either the staff tire of continued interference and quit their jobs, or the founder decides that, since he or she is doing the jobs that others are being paid to do, they might as well let the staff go and save the payroll costs. The boss then typically reverts to hero mode and the cycle repeats itself.

THE STRATEGIST MODE

A business founder is firmly in the strategist zone of activity when they are able to devote a significant part of their time to two of the fundamental management tasks defined by Drucker already mentioned:

- making today's business better
- and fashioning a new business for tomorrow

What exactly is "significant" is hard to quantify. As each business is unique, so the demands on the owner/manager's time will vary. That said, a minimum of a day a week sets a realistic basic threshold, to give you sufficient time to think, reflect and plan. Some people prefer to do this at work, others out of the office where they are less likely to be interrupted. Either way, the trick is to make yourself less available, away from the constant distraction of demands on your time. While many, more enlightened, business founders are happy to invest in the development and training of their staff, they are notoriously reluctant to invest in their own development – which is, when you think of it, bizarre, since the one person who is likely to have the greatest impact on the progression of the business is the one who owns and manages it! Those who *do* sign up to development programmes such as BGP will tend to identify two unexpected benefits that arise from being out of the office. First, physical separation helps them see their own business more sharply and objectively. Distance abstracts them from the daily routine and enables them to question assumptions which have never gone unchallenged before. Second, they are surrounded by others just like them. Every business may indeed be unique, but the managerial issues are common across all types. It is often remarked that it's easier to offer solutions to other people's business issues than it is to solve your own, and in our experience that is generally true. In addressing other people's challenges, however, you often shed light on your own.

FIRST THINGS FIRST

In terms of priority, it makes sense to spend that thinking time first on improving today's business. There is little point in planning for tomorrow's business before you have addressed improvements in the way the business currently operates. By analogy, you wouldn't extend a house if the foundations were shaky. In the previous two chapters we looked at two critical areas of any ambitious business, market development and financial management, where serious scrutiny is likely to uncover room for improvement. Some of those improvements are about the internal workings of the business, sorting out the plumbing and wiring if you like, so that processes such as invoice to cash and purchase to payment run as smoothly as possible, and are largely automated and independent of any one individual. There is nothing more irritating if a key process cannot be completed because someone is ill or on holiday. Other improvements are about securing the business from foreseeable risks, such as external scams or fraud perpetrated internally. And better outcomes are also about reining in the impulse to do things for which the business is unsuited or unprepared, such as premature diversification into products, services or markets which you don't properly understand.

When you are satisfied that the current issues in the business are fixed, and that the foundations are strong enough to support future growth, there are three key areas which will repay your time spent as a strategist many times over:

STUDYING THE COMPETITION

- Earlier in this book we introduced you to Nick Jenkins, founder of Moonpig.com. From the outset, Nick set great store by analysing and measuring data. As the business grew, he was able to demonstrate to investors that the cost of acquiring customers was steadily reducing and that gross margins were improving. He also studied his competitors' activities closely. Like many business pioneers, Moonpig had attracted other entrants and Nick bought their products every month as part of his market monitoring. By tracking the serial numbers printed on the cards he received, Nick realised that a TV campaign had dramatically increased the number of cards sold by a certain competitor from one month to the next. So Moonpig went on TV, with a cheap, more or less home-made campaign. Within weeks it had paid for itself. The company then doubled its TV spend with the same result, and doubled again. Eventually the company's advertising budget hit £1 mn as the formula was repeated over and over.

We will come back to the topic of finding and capitalising on that magic growth recipe later in the book.

BENCHMARKING YOUR FIRM AGAINST THE BUSINESSES YOU ASPIRE TO COMPETE AGAINST

• Most founders will compare themselves against their immediate competitors, but those who really think strategically for the longer term will also set their sights on businesses in the next division up. When Karan Bilimoria founded Cobra Beer he wanted not just to fill a gap in the market by brewing a better beer to accompany curry, but to build a famous brand. By entering a niche market like the tandoori restaurant sector Cobra was to a large extent protected, but Karan's aspirations were to build a really significant, multi-channel business. In 2003, when Cobra was still focused on the restaurant sector, Karan engaged the services of Team Saatchi, a division of advertising legends Saatchi & Saatchi. It was an unusual move for a business of Cobra's size, but Karan had registered that big, successful beer brands like Guinness, Heineken and Stella were defined in the public consciousness through the image created by their advertising. And if Cobra was going to punch above its weight as a brand, it needed the creativity and professionalism of the best in the advertising business.

Studying the businesses you aspire to compete against will give you a much surer grasp on the factors behind their success – and what you need to do to join their ranks.

PAYING ATTENTION TO YOUR OWN EFFECTIVENESS AS A LEADER

- This is how BGP participant Alex Fagioli has learned to max-imise his own productivity and impact as a business leader:

"It [the revelation] happened while I was on a plane to New York. I'd been working incredibly hard and felt that I was getting nowhere. I was incredibly frustrated. It was then I decided there had to be a bet-ter way." Alex Fagioli

Today [mid 2023] Alex is CEO of international cybersecurity firm Intragen, a job for which he was headhunted by its private equity backers. When he took part in BGP in 2013, it was as co-founder and chief executive of IT services company Tectrade. He joined the programme, he says, because he felt that after nearly 15 years of co-leading a business with virtually no management training, it was time to invest in himself. Alex's focus during BGP was on creating the growth plan that would enable him and his fellow founders to sell the company at the desired value. In fact, the business outperformed the plan and Alex comfortably achieved the financial independence he sought. Coming as he did from a modest background in South Africa, the importance of this was enormous. But it didn't quite turn out as expected. "Be careful what you wish for," says Alex. "I was a better CEO than golfer! What I really liked doing was building businesses. I bought the Porsche, but, like the golf clubs, it stayed in the garage." He also quickly realised that he liked being the CEO and struggled to work in a corporate structure.

As a result of BGP and his own reading and research, Alex had seri-ously engaged in improving his own personal effectiveness. He is deeply opposed to the notion of multi-tasking – in fact, he believes it's impossible and, if it's habitual, the evidence suggests it reduces managerial performance by up to 20%. Instead, he argues you should focus on one thing at a time, giving it your total attention and that incremental gains, as per the Japanese credo of Kaizen, yield lasting benefits. For Alex, managing time has evolved into a broader philoso-phy of how to live your life to the best effect. Every day, wherever he is in the world, he starts the morning with 20 minutes of transcen-dental meditation, followed by 70 minutes of exercise – including 10 minutes of stretching – before starting work. In the evening, whenever he can, he is back home for dinner with his family.

Alex's regime is based on a simple ordering of priorities. First, comes good mental health. Next, good physical health. Then family, and finally work. Good mental and physical health are a precursor to a good family life. If you get these first three right, the fourth – work – comes naturally.

At the office, he follows a similarly disciplined routine. With a mindset of setting himself up for a successful week, Alex knows where he's at risk of being overloaded and can move things around if he needs to, adhering to the principle of focusing on one thing at a time. To manage his workload, he follows the code of four Ds. When a task crosses his desk he determines:

First, whether it can be _dumped_, i.e. as being of no value to himself or the company.

Second, if not dumped then _delegated_ to someone else: "I say no to virtually everything. I value my time at £x00 per day. If it's not worth £x00 per day, I delegate the task or outsource it."

Third, can I or should I _do it now_, if it's sufficiently urgent and important?

Fourth, can I decide to _do it later_, and schedule time accordingly?

It may sound clinical, but Alex maintains that he has to hold himself to the highest possible standards if he is to run a high-performing business. His philosophy is that accountability at work starts with the individual: you are accountable first to yourself, to do your job to the best of your ability, then to your colleagues, and then to the company. To walk the talk, at the end of every week Alex rates his own performance and makes the results known to the rest of the team. "There is no room for mediocrity. If a person is consistently underperforming, that can impact twenty colleagues or more. Those people between them could be supporting 110 people, including themselves. If you ask me to choose between one underperformer and 110 other people, I'll choose 110 every time. My primary duty of care is always to the company."

Results suggest that Alex's approach is delivering. Intragen is expanding fast, with offices in London and four European countries. Meanwhile, Alex is very happy driving a Mini and the golf clubs are gathering dust in the garage!

Source: Alex Fagioli, Presentation 2022, updated June 2023

THE JOURNEY TOWARDS STRATEGIST

As anyone who has tried to kick an addictive habit such as smoking knows, changing one's behaviour is one of the hardest tasks to set yourself. If what you have read so far has convinced you that you need to allocate your time differently in order to achieve your ambitions, it's important to manage your own expectations of how far and how fast you can go. Behavioural change is a process, not an event, and it's unrealistic to expect it to happen overnight. Human beings are social animals and most of us, if we are planning a major change in our lives, will prefer to do this in the company of other people – hence the continuing popularity of organisations like Weightwatchers and other slimming clubs. If you wanted to take up a new pastime such as outdoor swimming, for example, you would most likely join a club where you would benefit from mutual support as well as challenge. The business founder by and large treads a lonely road and that is why programmes like BGP have grown in number to provide that camaraderie. There are, however, some small, less daunting steps which any ambitious business founder/owner can take to move themselves in the direction of becoming a strategist:

FOOD FOR THOUGHT #9

Behavioural change isn't easy, but it is possible. Here are four initiatives that you can try:

Four little words: "what would you do?"

The behavioural diagnostics we use tell us that most owner-managers display the characteristics of *both* hero *and* meddler. As a first step, then, we advise resisting the temptation to solve problems brought to you – the classic response of the hero. Greet the request with these four little words, and the questioner will usually tell you exactly what they would do. If it's a routine enquiry, nine times out of ten it's exactly what you would do too. Repeat this response often enough, and people will soon get the *overt* message: don't bother me with things you already know the answer to. Fairly quickly they'll also get the *implicit* message: *you* take responsibility for matters within *your* discretion. And the number of requests for heroic intervention will gradually decline until the problems that people bring genuinely are the exceptional ones.

Clarify roles, responsibilities and accountabilities

It's a lot less easy to justify meddling if there's clarity over who is supposed to be doing what. Often this is no more than a matter of writing things down, in consultation with key members of staff, so that everyone has a sharper understanding of their roles. This process can frequently bring to light misunderstandings or ambiguities, so is worth doing in its own right.

Delegate, don't abdicate

Don't try to move too far, too fast. Delegate a few, simple things, be available to support your staff and see how it goes. As their confidence builds, so you can up the responsibility. We know from research that owner-managers who grow their businesses successfully spend significant time coaching and mentoring their top teams.

Get out more

Yes, it's as simple as that. Spend less time in the office getting in other people's hair. Divorce yourself from the daily routine so you have more time and space in which to think. Many former BGP participants tell us that their best ideas for developing and growing the business come to them on the golf course, over dinner, in the bath – anywhere but in the office. People who get out more invariably discover two things:

- The office can indeed run without their permanent physical presence.
- People will not only embrace responsibility when they have to take decisions: those with talent and commitment will positively enjoy it.

Extracted from *From Brand Me to Brand Business* © David Molian 2023

BUT BE REALISTIC

At the same time, it's important to be realistic about how much of your time can be given over to the strategist role. Try to divorce yourself *completely* from the day-to-day running of the business, and you are likely to feel you no longer have the finger on the pulse of the business. Managing your diary – as per Alex Fagioli's example above – will ensure that you have the time available to give your customers, suppliers and staff the care and attention they need. The founder is inevitably the public face of the business, and this "ambassadorial" role is a critical one. Who would have predicted the rise of the celebrity plumber? Yet Pimlico Plumbers is one of the most high-profile British entrepreneurial success stories of recent years, set up in 1979 and sold by its founder Charlie Mullins in 2021 for a sum well north of £100 mn. In the latter years of his ownership, Mullins had become a frequent guest on TV talk shows, promoting his business alongside airing his opinions – but he also made a point of going out regularly to visit customers and sort out their leaking toilets!

THE IMPORTANCE OF THE TEAM

If there is one truth of business-building that cannot be emphasised enough, it is this: the senior team that you recruit and retain will build your business for you. Get the right people on the right seats on the bus and steer it in the right direction, and you will hugely increase your chances of reaching the destination of choice. The stories you read in the media of heroic entrepreneurs who build empires more or less single-handedly make engrossing news copy – but behind these men and women stand an army of great managers who have played a vital role in delivering those success stories. Some of the best business founders we know have acknowledged the contributions of their senior teams not just in words but by their deeds: when one BGPer who prefers to remain anonymous sold his cleanroom supplies business in 2006, he made a point of paying off the mortgages of those who had made it possible.

The intensifying war for talent means it will only get harder to attract the right people, so it will become increasingly crucial to make your business an attractive place to work. David Stone [BGP 2005], founder of semiconductor recruitment business MRL Consulting Group, started to pioneer the four-day working week several years ago. He was interviewed on the BBC in 2021 about his motivation for doing this and the impact on the firm's performance. Far from being a gimmick, David argues that his staff value the flexibility this brings and that no one tries to take unfair advantage. It is seen as a benefit, not a right, and has had no downside effects on client service. On the contrary, he maintains that morale and productivity, both of which he regularly measures, have gone up and the business continues its robust growth. A four-day working week might not suit every firm, but many BGP businesses have re-organised themselves so that work finishes by lunchtime on Fridays, with extra cover arranged as needed.

Bringing in the expertise you need to free up your time does not always entail new full-time hires at large salaries. There are other effective options. Some founders find interim bridging solutions, especially in the Finance and Marketing functions. The rise in agencies such as the FD Centre makes it possible to import high-level experience for a few days a month at variable cost and with limited commitment.

ACCELERANTS

Make yourself accountable: History shows the fate of those who believed in the divine right of kings. No one is infallible. In the way described above by Alex Fagioli, the best bosses find a way of holding themselves to account for their performance.

Offer people a career, not just a job: The best way of attracting the people who will help you build the business is by offering them a long-term opportunity, not simply a job. Smaller businesses can rarely compete with the salaries and perks offered by larger firms, but they do have one advantage – a smaller, less hierarchical organisation and thus the prospect of faster career progression. An experienced HR professional can advise on how to create and implement such programmes.

Reward your team little and often: Most businesses, certainly large ones, reward performance through bonuses paid annually. It's a routine mechanism, easy to administer and utterly without imagination. If it's your business, why not take the opportunity to do things differently? It costs nothing to say thank you, and not much more to thank someone's partner or spouse with a box of chocolates for allowing your member of staff to work overtime or at the weekend. When you hit a significant milestone, celebrate success in style. Founder of Pacific Direct Lara Morgan [BGP 1999] took her entire team to Barbados when company profits hit £1 mn. She also got considerable press coverage.

Beef up your advisors: We've talked before about reviewing the circle of advisers, the lawyers, bankers and accountancy firms you surround yourself with. What is their network of clients and associates? Do they have the kind of client and contacts base that will actively assist your business into the next division, or is it time to look elsewhere?

BLOCKERS AND BEARTRAPS

Don't play secret squirrel: You can't expect people to follow you with whole-hearted commitment if they don't know where you – or they – are going. Yet many owner-managers are obsessively secretive about their businesses, disclosing as little as possible. They don't share their business plans – even if they have one – and utterly resist any transparency about the firm's financial performance. A culture of secretiveness is fertile ground for breeding rumours and high staff turnover.

Don't recruit in your own image: We tend to be drawn towards people who are like us, but the business may well need individuals with utterly different skill sets and personalities. Recruitment specialist Rod Leefe [BGP 2000], who sold his firm Witan Jardine in 2008, points out that hiring at the senior level is like investing in a major business asset. You would think long and hard about purchasing a major piece of plant or machinery, and the same principle should be applied to top team recruitment.

Failing to invest in your "human capital": In the modern age, all businesses ultimately succeed or fail in direct proportion to the quality of their people. Yet there are still a few, otherwise enlightened, business owners, who fear that if they invest in training their staff, their employees will promptly defect to the competition. In a world of ever-tighter labour shortages, what is likely to happen if you *don't* invest in the skills and competences of your workforce? And, by the same token, if *you* don't continue to learn and develop as a leader?

SUMMARY

In this chapter we have analysed the ways in which ambitious business founders/owners spend their time, and the need to review and modify these as the requirements of the business change over time:

- The transition to sustainable growth requires a fundamental change in the mindset of the founder/owner. He or she must free themselves from the everyday demands of the business to give them the time and space to work *on* the business, not *in* it.
- That transition is unlikely to happen overnight. Changing one's behaviour is difficult and takes time and practice. Establishing a baseline helps: are you predominantly an artisan, a hero, a meddler, or on your way to becoming truly a strategist?
- Working on the business means making today's business better and fashioning a new business ready for the demands of tomorrow. Chapters one and two have provided the basis for beginning that process of making improvements in two areas of fundamental importance, market strategy and financial management, which will enhance today's business and build a solid foundation for future growth.
- Working on the business also frees up time for two vital tasks: studying and learning from the competition; and benchmarking your business against the businesses you aspire to become.
- Pay attention to your own effectiveness as a leader. The best lead by example. Are the standards you set yourself really those of a high-performing leader, or could you do better?

- Your team will deliver your business ambitions if you allow them to. They can only do so if you share your vision, your plans and create the environment in which they can perform to the best of their abilities.

NOTES

1 If you are interested in exploring these models further, three of the best-known are referenced at the end of this chapter.
2 In some cases, applicants are advised that their businesses are not developed enough to benefit from the programme.

FURTHER READINGS

Early growth models of business growth and development:

Steinmetz: first outlined at: www.sciencedirect.com/science/article/abs/pii/0007681369901074

Greiner: explained at: https://getlucidity.com/strategy-resources/guide-to-greiners-growth-model/

Lewis & Churchill: see https://hbr.org/1983/05/the-five-stages-of-small-business-growth

Lara Morgan, *More balls than most: Juggle your way to success with proven company shortcuts*, Infinite Ideas, 2011.

On the mindset and culture of high-performing organisations, drawing lessons from Motorsport, see www.linkedin.com/pulse/leadership-reflections-from-behind-multiple-lens-formula-one/ [with acknowledgments to Richard Parsons]

CHALLENGE TO GROWTH NUMBER FOUR: SUSTAINABLE POINTS OF DIFFERENCE
OR IF YOU'RE NOT BETTER OR DIFFERENT, WHAT RIGHT DO YOU HAVE TO PLAY IN YOUR MARKET?

INTRODUCTION

Every so often in its history a business is likely to face some sort of existential crisis, when it is forced to question why it does what it does, and whether there is a future in what it is doing. This type of crisis can be triggered by any number of factors, from the most mundane – we're running out of cash – to the most fundamental, such as tectonic shifts in consumer behaviour or technology that render the business obsolete. At such points, the business is forced to confront two harsh but telling questions:

- if we didn't exist, would anyone bother to re-create us?
- if we vanished tomorrow, would anyone miss us?

If the answer to both of these questions is clearly "no", those running the business have to do some serious thinking. In the first chapter, *Stick to the Knitting*, we cited two corporations, Wang and Commodore, which enjoyed a brief heyday as go-to

DOI: 10.4324/9781003410614-5

US computer brands in the 1980s but were casualties of the brutal battle for supremacy in the technology wars of the time. You could add Sinclair and Amstrad to the UK list. Business history is littered with the corpses of firms that either could not survive the intensity of competition or simply ceased to have a reason to exist. In chapter two, *Money, Money, Money*, we told the story of Patisserie Valerie, which at the time of writing had reduced to 42 outlets in the UK, the same brand but under new ownership. At the height of its success in 2018 the firm had nearly 200 shops and employed roughly 2500 people. It took less than four months for the firm to go from a high-profile, high street success to calling in the administrators. The downfall of Patisserie Valerie, of course, was caused by fraud, and its story serves as a reminder of the need for constant vigilance. However, the point we are making is the swiftness with which a business can go from golden child to orphan: today's brand is a shrunken shadow of its former self. Patisserie Valerie might have been missed, but not that much.

In this chapter we will explore what it takes for a growing business to maintain its purpose: to be better or different from its rivals, or indeed a combination of both. Through standing out from the competition, you will assert your continuing right to play in your market[s].

BEING BETTER

FOOD FOR THOUGHT #10

December 31st, 2019 will chiefly be remembered as the date when the outbreak of Covid in Wuhan, China, first came to world attention. In Adam Nemenyi's [BGP 2018] case, however, the news brought not so much anxiety as an overwhelming sense of relief. Earlier that same month he had finally sold his business, Aerospares 2000, in the face of contrary advice from many other people. Adam had ignored their voices and his judgment had been vindicated: as he put it, he was "on the last flight out of Dodge" [City].

He describes himself as not exactly a model school pupil. Academic subjects frustrated him, and he was motivated only by topics he considered to have a practical application. But he had two things going for him. First, he came from a family with a strong history of entrepreneurship. Family dinners, he says, were more like board meetings. Second, from an early age he had a passion for aviation and would go on to acquire a pilot's licence. When he enrolled as an undergraduate on a business studies sandwich course Adam spent his year out working in an aircraft parts firm, building an encyclopaedic knowledge of the industry. It was to prove an invaluable asset when he came to found his own company, Aerospares 2000, in 2003, and turn his passion into a successful business.

The basis of the new venture was Adam's belief that he could solve an urgent problem better than existing providers. In his opinion, too many business founders make the mistake of chasing the money rather than providing a differentiated solution to a customer's problem. Every minute that an aircraft is sitting on the ground, unable to move because a part needs replacing, is costing the operator thousands of pounds.

Incumbent suppliers might provide that spare within the hour. Adam's alternative vision was that Aerospares would have the part already on site, available for immediate collection: a compelling value proposition. His experience in the industry had also taught him the applicability of the Pareto principle, or 80/20 rule. He knew which spare parts were in greatest demand, the length of replacement cycles, and was able to organise his buying and stockholdings accordingly. Adam combined that knowledge with a relentless focus on efficiency and driving out costs. Unsurprisingly, he was able to grow a business delivering impressive margins of 20–25%.

Adam had created a textbook example of the BGP recipe for growth: find a niche in which you have a sustainable advantage and go all out to dominate it.

Source: Presentation 2022

By the time Adam enrolled on the BGP he had already made that transition from artisan, with his comprehensive knowledge of aircraft spares, all the way through to strategist: he had solved the problem of the business being critically dependent on him, the founder, by transferring the knowledge in his head to a computerised database, and by recruiting a highly competent team. He joined the BGP to develop himself as a leader, but his main focus, as it turned out, was the preparation of Aerospares for a future sale. We will return to follow his story later in this book. In the meantime, however, it is worth examining the factors which made his business an outstanding one, able to yield margins that out-performed the industry average.

- He had made himself the "go to" person in the industry, a reference point for his customer base. That arose from Adam's sheer passion for flying and was supplemented by the countless hours of groundwork which he had put in early in his career. If there is an opportunity to become the recognised authority in your sector of the market, take it.
- Adam identified the point of pain felt most acutely by his customers, and mobilised whatever resources he could lay his hands on to solve it. The Aerospares proposition is simple and easily conveyed: we have the part that you need, and you can have it faster from us than from anyone else.

- His apprenticeship in the industry had taught him the fundamentals of stock management, turnover rates, demand and replacement cycles. At first sight it seems remarkable that the larger incumbents in the aircraft spares industry did not organise themselves in the way that Aerospares did, to exploit the same opportunity which Adam had spotted. In fact, this is relatively common in big markets, where established corporations have a tendency to atrophy into sluggish, process-driven bureaucracies – we have seen many agile BGP businesses take advantage of what established competitors have failed to see.

- Exceptional margins often result from understanding the difference between *cost* and *value*. The value of a spare part vastly outweighs its cost if a plane is losing its operator many thousands of pounds for every hour that it cannot fly.

BEING DIFFERENT

FOOD FOR THOUGHT #11

Pacific Direct Ltd [now ADA Pacific Direct] was founded in 1991 by Lara Morgan, following a chance encounter in her home city of Hong Kong. She was approached by a hotel supplies manufacturer to see if she would represent them as a sales agent in the UK, to which she was relocating. Lara knew nothing about the hotel industry, sewing kits or toiletries, but she knew quite a lot about printing and production processes. Above all, from her time spent working for Yellow Pages, she knew how to sell.

Her first port of call in the UK was the Dorchester Hotel. Having seen the sewing kit samples shown them by Lara, the Head of Housekeeping placed an order for 5000. Lara accepted, with no idea how she was going to meet the order but absolutely determined not to let the customer down. At the end of the first year of trading, Pacific achieved a turnover of £300,000. Over the next 18 months the firm developed its own range of house brands for the hotels market, designed to look and feel like premium fragranced products. By 1996 sales had increased to £2.25 mn, helped by the company's range expansion into slippers, soaps, shower gels and other hotel amenities. Most customers had no idea that the business was run for the first three years from Lara's kitchen table and then from a Victorian villa on a main road in Bedford.

Lara described herself as driven, highly competitive [she had played lacrosse at international level for England, swam five miles a week and ran triathlons] and bolshy. She refused to take no for an answer and was determined to create a business that reflected her own style, in stark contrast to her larger, more staid competitors. Lara once sent an empty cardboard box to a recalcitrant potential customer, containing a note that read: "*If you place an order with us I'll send you a full one!*" Pacific's culture was more than gimmickry, however. The commitment to customer service was absolute. When a lorry carrying a delivery crashed into the side of a hotel it was supplying in Scotland, Pacific offered to have a plumber on the scene in an hour and sent flowers with an apology for the hotel owners – even though the vehicle was owned and operated by a contractor.

Inside the business, Lara created a culture that was heavily sales-focused and performance-based. Her first recruit expressed a desire to drive a BMW. Rather than giving her a company car, Lara made it possible for her to achieve this through hitting sales and profit targets by her own efforts. There was minimal hierarchy and bureaucracy was non-existent. Meetings were kept as short as possible and focused on sales, profitability, innovation and the tracking of competitors. Within three years the company

> was profitable, and the margins reflected the upmarket customer base of quality hotels.
>
> Lara maintained that her unorthodox management style was the result of naivety. In any case, Pacific certainly started to attract attention and in late 1996, just four years after starting, Lara received her first offer to buy the company.
>
> Source: company case study

In fact, Lara rejected this approach ["Pacific was worth much, much more"] and went on to sell the business when it was substantially larger, twelve years later, in 2008. When she took part in the BGP in 2000 she had taken Pacific into the airlines sector and acquired licences to sell top-of-the-range brands such as the British perfume house Penhaligon's. However, at this stage of her journey she was still oscillating between the hero and meddler modes of behaviour, and desperate to free herself from the routine but necessary admin tasks that she loathed. On the plus side, she had laid the groundwork for creating a truly exceptional business that stood out in its marketplace.

Even from this condensed history, it should be evident that Pacific Direct was a very different kind of company:

- By starting at the very top of the market, Lara conveyed a clear message to every subsequent customer: if we're good enough for the Dorchester, we're good enough for you.
- Sourcing from Hong Kong/China is commonplace today. In 1991 it was still comparatively rare. This combination of high quality plus low cost was extremely compelling. The very name the business traded under drove home the proposition.
- The cosmetics business into which Lara diversified, and which was to dominate Pacific in its later years, has long been driven by charismatic, larger-than-life female founders – think

Esteé Lauder, Helena Rubenstein and Elizabeth Arden, to name but three. Anita Roddick, the entrepreneur behind the Body Shop, is probably the best-known recent British example. Lara Morgan fitted the mould.

- This is a very competitive industry. Those businesses founded by the pioneers of yesteryear had morphed into giant multinationals, with huge advertising budgets and manufacturing economies of scope and scale. Agility and responsiveness to customers' needs was pretty much the only basis on which Pacific Direct could differentiate itself.

INSIDER OR OUTSIDER?

The question is often asked if it is a disadvantage to be a newcomer to an industry in which you are going to start and grow a business, or whether there are actually benefits. From what we have observed, being an outsider rarely puts a brake on growth. Before they entered the chocolate market, Angus Thirlwell and his business partner Peter Harris had worked as colleagues for a small computer hardware business in Cambridge. A major attraction of moving into confectionery was that it had none of the problems associated with the technology sector. Karan Bilimoria had qualified as both an accountant and a lawyer before starting Cobra Beer. His perspective on the beer market was as a customer and enthusiastic consumer of curries. What he couldn't find was exactly the right beer to accompany his favourite cuisine: a brew with the depth of an ale, easy to drink, but without the gassiness of a lager. After months of experimentation with the help of one of India's top master brewers in Bangalore, he perfected the recipe. From the outset, Cobra was a distinctively different brand. There is also something to be said for the old adage that in the country of the blind, the one-eyed man is king. When Nick Jenkins developed his plan for Moonpig in 1998, he knew nothing about this embryonic thing called the internet. But, as he himself said, nobody else did either. What Nick Jenkins *did* know was that the emerging technology created an opportunity to create a personalised greetings card which did not exist before, and that this was a business that could be scaled up into something very significant.

From these examples and many others we have followed, two conclusions emerge. One, that there are transferable skills which ambitious business founders can bring to bear when they enter unfamiliar markets. Angus Thirlwell and Peter Harris between them had significant experience in sales, marketing, brand management and business systems. Lara Morgan knew how to sell, and she understood both print and production, vital for packaging. Two, it is possible to learn "on the go" what you need to know if you are sufficiently driven and passionate about the business. Karan Bilimoria was a dissatisfied customer who was convinced he knew exactly what was missing from the tandoori restaurant beverages offer and was confident that there were enough people like him to invest six months of his time in perfecting a solution in India.

On the other hand, in a highly technical sector such as aircraft spares, the deep knowledge that derives from a long apprenticeship is an enormous competitive asset – and one that is hard to replicate from a standing start. By the time he was ready to set up Aerospares, Adam Nemenyi says that he knew in detail the specifications of thousands of spare parts and the frequency with which they were needed by air operators.

CHALLENGERS AND CONTRARIANS

These "personal assets" – such as transferable skills, the capacity to learn rapidly on the job and the almost obsessive understanding that comes from a passion for something – provide the foundations for creating a business that is better or different, or both. It is part of the leader's job to embed these qualities of versatility, agility and enthusiasm within the business so that the entity eventually stands apart from the founder: a Brand Business enterprise, rather than a Brand Me business, to revert to the

Table 4.1 Hotel Chocolat: strategy linked to core values

We are	*We are not*
Leaders	*Followers*
Adders of value through our ideas	*Wage slaves to other companies*
Always seeking to improve	*Red tape merchants*
Exciting, excited and excitable	*Dull and predictable*
Building something worthwhile	*Short-termist*
Driven by our vision and teamwork	*Driven by fear and politics*

Source: company presentation 2004

concept introduced in a previous chapter. Hotel Chocolat's co-founders explicitly linked the qualities and values of the business to its strategy as above.

Staff and new recruits were left in no doubt about what the business stood for. That manifesto was made concrete when, after nearly two years of painstaking research, the company finished rebranding itself as Hotel Chocolat and opened its first store in Watford in 2003. It unequivocally set out its stall as a *challenger* business. The term is used of new entrants to a well-established market sector who offer customers a proposition that is starkly different from what is offered by the established players. The British mass chocolate market had been formed by the big domestic manufacturers such as Cadbury's, Rowntree's and Fry's, whose origins dated back to the 19th century. Their recipes were formulated mainly around milk varieties and tended to contain higher levels of sugar and processed fat, and lower levels of cocoa butter: they catered, essentially, for the British sweet tooth. European chocolate-makers on the other hand favoured dark varieties, less sweet, and with a higher cocoa butter content.

The UK market had long been divided between the mass milk segment dominated by British producers selling through corner shops and supermarkets, and the premium segment supplied by continental producers, distributed through specialist upmarket shops as well as mainstream retailers. In the British mass market one chain of specialist retailers, the family-owned

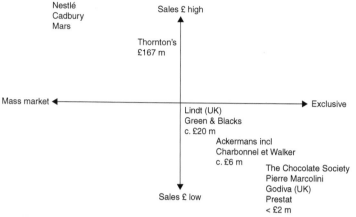

UK total chocolate confectionery market: £3.6 billion

UK boxed assorted chocolates: £552 m

Figure 4.1 UK Chocolate Market, 2003, Brand Mapping.
Source: the author

Thornton's, was dominant with its own-manufactured brand, sold through hundreds of stores across the country. At the time Hotel Chocolat opened its first store, Thornton's sales were £167 mn.

Co-founders Angus and Peter believed that the tastes of British consumers were changing. Low-cost travel to European countries had opened many more people's eyes and palates, and consumers' disposable incomes were bolstered by a steadily growing economy. A new opportunity was opening up, in the form of "mass premium": the democratisation of hitherto luxury foods. Hotel Chocolat would be in the vanguard. Market mapping demonstrates the opportunity.

The new entrant challenged the incumbent on numerous fronts:

- The first Hotel Chocolat outlet was opened more or less directly opposite a branch of Thornton's in Watford shopping centre. Purchasers of chocolate could make a direct comparison. As Angus said, "if we could make it work here, we felt confident that the concept was right".

- The orthodox view in the market was that the purchase of chocolate was highly seasonal. Consumers bought chocolate mainly in the winter and as gifts for special occasions. The trade press reported that Thornton's achieved 35% of its sales in the seven weeks leading up to Christmas, and around 10% in the run-up to Valentine's Day. To even out the trading pattern, Thornton's stocked ice cream for the summer season and trialled a number of in-store cafés across selected locations. Hotel Chocolat on the other hand knew from the success of the subscription-based Chocolate Tasting Club that people would buy chocolate all year round. Rather than diversifying, Hotel Chocolat focused on chocolate alone, introducing continual innovations that appealed throughout the year. Creative novelty encouraged buyers to keep coming back.

- The Thornton's proposition was essentially *transactional*: customers came into a store to make a purchase, and left. By comparison, the whole idea of Hotel Chocolat was *experiential*. "We want people to feel that they're checking in," said Angus. "It's an environment which they can step into outside normal, everyday life – a little dose of luxury in someone's day, if you like. It's more than just a shop."

- Staff were recruited for their enthusiasm and encouraged not only to know the product range but also to be able to answer questions about the production process and the provenance of the chocolates. [In fact, once the stores really took off, partner Peter Harris installed remote CCTV monitoring to head off callers or visitors from the company's head office from interrupting staff on days when a particular store was busy.]

- Products were sourced almost exclusively from overseas suppliers, with a bias towards dark chocolate and a distinctive taste profile. The cocoa butter content was kept high across the price points and new product introductions had to pass a stringent process of review before they could be placed on the shelves.

Within three years the company had four stores in the east of England. Today it has around 100 branded outlets and sells through John Lewis, Waitrose and other supermarkets. In 2006 the firm purchased the rundown Rabot Estate in St Lucia, regenerated it, and now sells single-source products from its own plantation. In 2011 it opened its own hotel, Boucan, on the Rabot Estate and in 2013 set up two cafés cum restaurants, one in Leeds and the other in Borough Market, London. At the time of writing, Hotel Chocolat has revenues of £226 mn and is listed on the Stock Exchange. Thornton's has closed all its retail stores and sells online and through supermarkets. Since 2015 the company has been owned by Luxembourg-based Ferrero. In June 2022 Thornton's reported sales of £86.5 mn and made a loss.

Which one is now the challenger brand?

THE CONTRARIAN BUSINESS

The challenger business shares many similarities with the *contrarian* business, an enterprise which sets out to be different from the pack. Nick Jenkins' working name for his business pre-launch was Splat!, but he discovered it was already registered. He could have chosen to call the business something like "The Great British Greetings Card Company" but, he says, it would

Table 4.2 Challenger and contrarian shared similarities

Dimension	Challenger	Contrarian
Market Entry		
Operating Style	√	√
Customer Service	√	√
Communications	√	√

have been instantly forgettable. *Moonpig*, which happened to be a nickname Nick acquired at school, was short and memorable, especially when combined with the graphic of a pig wearing an astronaut's helmet. Likewise, Tristram and Rebecca Mayhew could have called their business "High Wire Adventures" or something on those lines: *Go Ape* is not only distinctively different but also subtly subversive, which appeals to people looking for something on the wilder side.

Our observations suggest the main dimension of difference is that of market entry. As noted above, challenger businesses enter established markets and throw down the gauntlet to the incumbents, much as Virgin Atlantic deliberately set itself up to compete against BA in the 1980s and 1990s. Contrarian businesses usually start as pioneers of new markets, where the major obstacle is convincing those who might block them that their ideas are possible – that received wisdom can be overturned.

The idea for Go Ape originated in a family holiday in France, when the Mayhews came across a high ropes course in France called *aventure de forêt*. The couple had been thinking of setting up a business of their own, and wondered whether the concept of a treetops obstacle course embedded in a forest setting could be transferable to the UK. At the time – the early 2000s – there was no comparable established industry, just a few solo zipwire operators who had set up in fields or quarries. The biggest hurdle the couple foresaw was a prevailing health and safety culture which could make operating the concept too difficult. To their surprise, they found an unexpected ally in the form of the Royal Society for the Prevention of Accidents [RoSPA], which actively encouraged them to go ahead. RoSPA had formed the view that an excessive emphasis on health and safety was preventing children from learning to live with the challenges of the natural world. Provided Go Ape could demonstrate that they could assure visitor safety, they would receive RoSPA's backing. And so at a time when schools were banning children from playing conkers, Go Ape swam against the tide and got into the business of encouraging people, in their own words, to live life adventurously.

This resistance to being told that something is too difficult or impossible was also the trigger for the worldwide business that is Topgolf. The Jolliffe twins, Steve and Dave, believed that the humdrum golf driving range could be made immensely more attractive – and profitable – if it became a destination and entertainment venue. To unlock the potential, they needed to find a way of inserting a microchip into a golf ball, to record its movements and transmit these to a scoreboard. The brothers commissioned a technical consultancy to conduct a feasibility study. The report that came back said it was impossible. Steve and Dave were delighted: if experts said it couldn't be done, no one else would even try. They poured in the money they had made from a previous business venture to fund an R&D programme to prove the experts wrong and, sure enough, it could be done. After a lot of time and a great deal of money, in 2000 Topgolf opened its first venue in the Jolliffes' home town of Watford. Today there are 100 Topgolf venues worldwide, hosting 50 million visitors. To demonstrate Topgolf's contrarian credentials even more strongly, fewer than half of those visitors actually play golf, let alone visit a standard golf driving range!

There are examples of contrarian businesses to be found in the services sector as well. Rod Leefe [BGP 2001] was the majority shareholder and CEO of the accountancy recruitment firm Witan Jardine, which he sold to an overseas acquirer in 2008. There are an awful lot of recruitment firms specialising in the supply of accountants for permanent or interim appointments. After Rod took over as head of the firm he reviewed how he could differentiate the business from the competition more strongly.

The recruitment industry is notoriously sales-driven. The traditional business model is that most employees have a sales role and are rewarded partly by a base salary and partly by commission as a percentage of fees earned. In many firms, perhaps most, the resulting relationship with clients is essentially a transactional one: to revert to the distinction made in Chapter One, the prevailing culture is a *hunting* culture. The sales person closes the deal and moves on to the next opportunity.

Rod identified a gap in customer service that Witan Jardine could fill, by creating a new function of *farmers* within the firm. Their role was essentially that of account managers, to nurture long-term relationships with Witan Jardine's main clients: to review, for example, recruitment needs beyond the next quarter in the light of changes in the client's market sector. The aim was to offer informed guidance, with no expectation of an immediate return. In an industry focused almost exclusively on next week, it was not difficult to stand out. Witan Jardine's "farmers" were paid solely by salary, not commission, and their performance was assessed by a different set of metrics. Rod also introduced the concept of "first two". He did not expect that clients should always make Witan Jardine their first port of call when searching for candidates – this was frankly unrealistic. But he *did* expect that Witan Jardine would be on the receiving end of the first or second call. It was a way of measuring both how much the firm was in their clients' front of mind, and how well the farmers and hunters were working together to achieve the longer-term goal of building the business. This initiative was a major factor in an approach out of the blue from an Australian buyer looking for an outstanding British company to acquire.

CREATING A DISTINCTIVE CULTURE

In Table 4.2 we identified that operating style, customer service and communication are all common features of businesses that fall into the categories of challenger or contrarian. These features combine to create a distinctive character or business culture. In the cases we've described it's difficult to separate the operating style from customer service because the one informs and blends into the other. In these firms, once they have proved themselves, the staff tend to be given a great deal of discretion and autonomy in how they operate their part of the business.

This in itself is something of a virtuous circle because the kind of people you'd like to attract to grow your business are exactly the people who value the discretion to do their job to the best of their ability. And it almost goes without saying that enthusiasm, engagement and a willingness to solve problems will normally correlate with a great customer experience.

To grow a business successfully it is not essential to set out with the aim of becoming a full-blown challenger or contrarian. But there are characteristics of such businesses you can adopt which will certainly assist the process. In the cases we've discussed, what we see emerging over time is the emergence of a *corporate personality*. These are businesses that have a distinctive character. As a customer of such firms, you have a very clear idea of who you are dealing with, which in turn creates a set of expectations.

In the previous chapter, we featured Alex Fagioli talking about the standards that he sets for himself as a leader as well as for his staff and his belief that he can only achieve and maintain these levels of performance through a well-disciplined personal regime. There are downsides as well as upsides to this constant striving to be among the best.

On the upside:

*   Your business should acquire a "fanbase" of loyal customers that will expand with the growth of the company. Imagine loyalty as a ladder. On the bottom rung are people who are indifferent to your company's goods and services or, worse, actively hostile and critical [and prepared to say so]. Social media provides the perfect environment for snipers to take aim at you. For many sectors, independent review sites such as TripAdvisor or Trust Pilot provide a running score on what people think of you. You might have a right of reply to challenge reviews or comments you believe to be untrue

or unfair, but often the damage is already done, and a public scrap rarely benefits anyone. Far better to focus on moving as many customers as possible to the topmost rung of the ladder, where they become your active advocates. Virtually all of Go Ape's promotion, for instance, is done by the visitors who upload films onto social media of their own days out at the company's sites.

• The creation of a business with an identity of its own is a necessary condition for a separation between the founder and the firm. The more clear blue water there is between you and the business, the more valuable the business is. You may *think* you will never want to sell your firm, but it is surely better to create more options, not fewer, as we will see in the next chapter.

On the downside:

• There is truth in the old saying that the higher you rise, the further you have to fall. Raising your head above the parapet makes it easier for people to take pot shots. Setting high standards means you have to live up to them. It's better not to make a promise than to fail to deliver it.

• We talked previously about the marathon that ambitious business founders run. Experienced long-distance runners maintain that preparation and planning are as essential as training. At regular intervals, competitors need to rehydrate, replenish their energy and break through the physical and mental barriers that scream "I've had enough". The stresses suffered by the business owner are comparable: many participants on the BGP have told us that an important motive for attending is that they have simply fallen out of love with their business because of the demands it makes on them. They are usually surprised when they find there are others who feel the same and are reassured to learn that there are remedies.

ACCELERANTS

Occupy the high ground. The most effective way to assume a commanding position in any market sector is to become an authority. Demonstrate that you are better or different by taking every opportunity to showcase your expertise: at conferences, exhibitions, in the trade press, on social media, on the television and airwaves. If you are offered a speaking opportunity, take it. If you hate public speaking, either learn how to do it or nominate others in the business who enjoy it. Develop thought-pieces and conduct research. Fill your website with useful content. Bear in mind the slogan "as seen on TV": it still carries weight. Everyone likes to be associated with a winner.

Pay careful attention to your physical and mental health. It is all too easy – especially for men – to dismiss such concerns. Many of us thrive under pressure, but constant and unrelenting pressure at some point turns into stress. Stress is neither trivial nor a sign of weakness, and the effects on those you care most about can be devastating. Fortunately, there is far greater awareness today of the risks and dangers of burn-out and plenty of professional advice to hand. In all likelihood, you will suffer from fatigue and days when the business you once delighted in seems like a millstone around your neck. That's okay – in fact, it's normal. The important thing is to remember that this too will pass.

Actively seek to recruit people who are better than you. *"Surround yourself with people who are smarter than you in different areas, then learn from them"*, says Emily Weiss, founder of billion-dollar cosmetics company, Glossier. Here is a simple test: when you walk into your place of work, do you raise or lower the average IQ? Generally speaking, our egos would like us to think of ourselves as the smartest people in the room. In reality, the smartest people in the room are usually those who recognise that they are *not* the smartest people in the room and are quite content with this. Consider this: if *you* are not employing people who are in some important respect better than you, then someone else is. Their employers may well be your competitors.

BEARTRAPS AND BLOCKERS

Beware the energy vampires. In many businesses there lurks at least one energy vampire. They can be recognised by their ability to depress everyone else's spirits and throw a dampener on all around them. When they walk into the room, the mood changes and enthusiasm just drains away. If you have a member of staff that you or others avoid because of their relentless negativity or capacity to waste your time, you have an energy vampire. Such people drag down the firm's momentum and make life difficult for their colleagues. You're the boss. If they can't change, the vampires have to go.

Don't substitute stunts for creating a healthy company culture. How often have you seen a big company's TV advertising and compared it with the grim reality of what you have experienced as a customer? [Travel businesses in particular take note]. In the search for being better or different, businesses sometimes latch onto tired gimmicks while failing to address underlying symptoms of cultural dysfunctionality. If good staff are leaving in droves there's no point in plastering the office with smiley posters and "zany" quotes.

SUMMARY

In this chapter we have explored the concept of creating sustainable points of difference: the imperative to provide a continuing stream of reasons for your business's right to play in its market[s]:

• In the more mature phase of a firm's growth, a major challenge is to sustain its relevance in the market. Why should customers continue to buy from you? Being better, different, or both provides a compelling reason.

- Being an insider or outsider in your market is less important than the ability to exploit your personal assets.
- Contrarian and challenger businesses often provide great models to learn from. Your business does not have to conform to either type to be successful, but there are valuable insights to be gained on how to do things better or differently to create a competitive edge.
- Creating a distinctive corporate style or personality is a primary task for the owner/leader of a business. Customers and suppliers know what you represent. Businesses that stand out from their peers will attract more interest from potential acquirers as well as tending to command greater loyalty from customers and staff alike.
- Assuming the role of an authority in your industry is an excellent way to differentiate yourself. However, the higher you rise, the further you have to fall. Hold yourself to the highest standards and keep your promises.

FURTHER READINGS

On challenger brands, see https://dash.app/blog/challenger-brand-examples

On contrarian brands, and contrarian thinking generally, see *The Rebel Entrepreneur: Rewriting the Business Rulebook*, Jonathan Moules, Kogan Page, available at www.amazon.co.uk/Rebel-Entrepreneur-Rewriting-Business-Rulebook/dp/0749464828

CHALLENGE TO GROWTH NUMBER FIVE: REINVENTING THE BUSINESS TO BUILD FURTHER VALUE
SHOULD I STAY OR SHOULD I GO?

INTRODUCTION

If you have successfully addressed and overcome the challenges outlined in Chapters One to Four, you are now the owner of an established business, with clear points of difference from the competition, and having built value that is – at least in part – independent of you. A team of capable managers is in place, some of whom should be better at what they do than you. The business is generating both cash and profit and – quite possibly after some time – you can draw a decent income from it. You are able finally to take leave from the business without constantly keeping tabs on what is going on back in the workplace. You may even have attracted the attention of potential acquirers, as Lara Morgan of Pacific Direct did, just five years after starting her business. Good growth businesses are always targets for bigger companies and private capital on the acquisition trail.

A knock comes at the door, followed by a proposal. At such moments, the owner/founder will inevitably ask themselves: does the equation stack up? Is what someone else prepared to pay right now enough recompense for the time,

DOI: 10.4324/9781003410614-6

money, blood, sweat and tears that I have poured into this business? Or, like Lara Morgan, will you decide that "[Pacific] was worth much, much more" and choose to continue?

In this chapter we explore the opportunities to create further value in your business as it enters a more mature phase and outline the options to realise that value through a full or partial exit.

THE NEED FOR REINVENTION

We opened Chapter 1 with the story of Belvoir Cordials, the family business behind the famous British soft drinks brand. As you may remember, we described the decision to diversify into the children's drinks segment at an early stage in the life of the company – an illustration of the dangers of departing too soon from the core business. All the evidence we have seen confirms that the optimal strategy for an ambitious business founder is to identify a market niche where there is unmet demand and to enjoy the protection that offers from the attention of bigger rivals. In Belvoir's case this was distribution through local farm shops and delicatessens. Going this route allows a business the time and space in which to develop its customer offer and to build the systems and structures that make it a viable enterprise. Out of this come opportunities to strengthen its position in the market through being better or different.

The selected niche market may be enough to sustain the growth of the business for a considerable time: Cobra Beer, for instance, concentrated on the tandoori restaurant market for a good decade. By then the brand was known well enough, promoted by a memorable series of TV campaigns, to secure favourable deals with mainstream distribution channels such as the major supermarkets. However, like Lara Morgan with Pacific Direct, Karan Bilimoria was confident that Cobra had much, much further to go, and had no desire to sell up so early in the life of the brand. Many business owners/managers who participate in programmes like the BGP share that ambition. They are confident that their businesses can be scaled further, creating far greater value, and that they have the abilities to take it on that journey. The challenge they now face is how to pursue those additional opportunities for growth without putting what they have built so far in jeopardy. That brings us back to the two fundamental questions which we posed at the outset of this book. For the *next* phase of the journey:

- Is the business able to scale?
- And is the boss capable of change?

In other words, can the business and its owner/manager be reinvented?

SHOULD I GO OR SHOULD I STAY?

As a typical example, take a growing business with a turnover at present of £5 mn, and a founder who believes, with good reason, that sales can be tripled or even quadrupled within five years. That additional revenue will come from selling more of what it currently does to existing customers, selling more of what it currently does to adjacent markets, and selling new products and services to existing customers [as per the Ansoff matrix presented at the start of Chapter 1]. The firm employs 30 staff today. To achieve these sales ambitions, the founder thinks she will have to double the headcount, the major increases being in the size of the salesforce, a bigger research and development unit, and an expanded logistics department to manage a more complex order fulfilment process.

It looks like the first question is answered: the business is indeed able to scale.

A major attraction of this strategy is that while sales should go up by three or four times, staff numbers only double. Productivity and value added per employee will thus increase dramatically. It will be a more efficient business, benefiting from economies of scale and scope, and by the same logic a much more valuable business in five years' time.

All this will require additional investment. It might be possible to do this through reinvesting funds generated by the business, but it means keeping a tight control on costs. That in turn implies keeping increases to staff wages low, and not offering the kind of salary packages that might be needed to attract new, well-qualified staff. The owner will have to limit her own drawings from the business, which means trimming her own family's lifestyle for a while longer. Alternatively, she could start returning the bank's emails and start a conversation about a commercial loan. The bank seems very keen to lend money on attractive terms to a business which is currently debt-free. The finance director thinks that the business could accommodate a loan facility of up to £1 mn without undue risk to its balance sheet. Until now the business has grown through its own resources, something of which the founder is proud: there are no interest payments and no obligations to any third party. But an injection of a million pounds could really accelerate the rate of progress and provide a safety cushion of cash. After all, what if Covid-19 or something like it were to come out of nowhere?

However, there's another dimension to Plan A, as the owner likes to call it, which concerns her. Some, perhaps a quarter, of the loyal staff who have been with the business from the start are almost certainly not the right people to play a leading part in a big leap forward. They have neither the skills nor experience required and probably little appetite for change. Either they will have to take subordinate positions to the new managers the owner plans to recruit or be eased out of the firm. These are not conversations that she is looking forward to having.

And then there is her own position. Does she have the personal stamina for another five years and the ability to lead a business which will look so different from what she knows and understands?

The answer to the second question of whether the owner is capable of change is maybe not so clear.

This illustrates the classic dilemma faced by ambitious business founders/owners in the more mature stage of their companies' lifecycle. At the start-up stage there is relatively little to lose. Five, six, seven years or more down the line, much more is at stake. Cash in on what you have – the sure outcome – or place your bets? Whichever way you go, there are risks. Sell up *in total* now, and you may regret that the acquiring party will reap all the future value which you could have harvested. Sell up *in part*, and you could regret the inevitable loss of autonomy that comes from working as an employee in what was **your** business. *Stay* with the business and you face the market, financial and unknowable risks described above, as well as the personal demands. On the Business Growth Programme we invite participants to visualise these different futures as explicitly as they can, to help them choose the outcome that will suit them as well as their business. One participant who decided that a partial sale was the right road to go down was Adam Nemenyi [BGP 2018], whose story we introduced in the previous chapter:

FOOD FOR THOUGHT#12

Within a short time of Adam's arrival on the BGP, the question was put to him: should he think seriously about a sale? Aerospares 2000 was unquestionably a prime candidate. In the six years between 2012 and 2017 the business had an unbroken record of sales and profits, trending upwards. The company carried no debt and Adam was the sole shareholder. Among its big-name clients were established airlines like BA and Virgin Atlantic and the more recent challengers like Easyjet, Wizzair and Jet2. The business was just moving into a newly commissioned headquarters cum warehouse, which mean that no big capital expenditure was on the horizon. A number of factors tipped the balance in favour of Adam's decision to seek a buyer for the majority of his shares:

- Over the past seventeen years, Aerospares had benefited greatly from the long upward growth cycle in

the airline industry, boosted by the rise of the low-cost sector. At some point this trend would peak and quite possibly turn down. The timing was as good as it was likely to get.
- The right investor/business partner would bring with them deep pockets and greater expansion opportunities.
- Adam's passion for the business was undiminished – he would happily continue as CEO.
- His personal wealth was tied up in the company. It was better to be a cash millionaire than a paper one.
- A close friend had recently passed away, causing Adam to review his own life and priorities.
- Not least, he had his own "magic number" in mind – though kept firmly to himself!

The "magic number" is the price at which a founder/owner is prepared to sell their business. We discuss this in detail later in the chapter.

Adam made the right call. A big, unexpected event in the form of Covid-19 turned out to be just around the corner. In the year after the sale of Aerospares 2000 to a private equity house was completed, the passenger airline business collapsed. The company's sales halved, and its profits were reduced by two-thirds. Throughout this period of market turmoil, the new parent remained highly supportive, agreeing with Adam that out of crisis new opportunities often arise. The business was cash-rich and able to purchase inventory at knock-down prices. Although almost all passenger aircraft were grounded, the cargo sector boomed, as international supply chains continued to operate. Aerospares invested significantly in this area, where it had previously had little presence. The business opened a new office in Dublin to service the aircraft leasing companies based in Ireland.

By 2021 the company's financial performance was back to that of 2019, and in 2022 revenues rose by over 50%. In that same year, Aerospares acquired an established aircraft spares business in the US, giving it a presence on both sides of the Atlantic. The combined revenues of the two businesses exceed $125 mn, making it now one of the largest in its industry. Adam remains CEO and has retained his residual shareholding. At some point in the future, the enlarged business will almost certainly be sold. Adam's philosophy is that it is better to have a small slice of a big pie, than a big slice of a small one.

STAYING WITH THE BUSINESS: MANAGING THE RISKS OF FURTHER EXPANSION

The circumstances of every business and its owner[s] are of course unique. Selling a business is not a decision to be taken lightly, and some who chose to do so live to regret it [the reasons for which we will also examine later in the chapter]. The single biggest challenge faced by those founders/owners who stick with it is managing the risks of expansion in their desire to take the business to the next level.

To paraphrase the late Donald Rumsfeld[1], former US Secretary of Defense, there are risks that are knowable and predictable, and risks that are very difficult or impossible either to predict or qualify: many natural or man-made disasters would fall into this category. Each of us responds to the prospect of risk differently, being more or less risk-averse, and the readiness to take business risk is weighed against the likelihood of its occurring and the size of the potential reward. It is impossible to eliminate all risks since we have no control over what cannot be anticipated, but *foreseeable* risks can be managed to a level that is acceptable. There are approaches to pursuing expansionary business strategies that we have seen work very effectively in practice, and which can serve as templates for other ambitious founders.

THE EVOLUTIONARY BUSINESS STRATEGY

This is the mode of growth that the majority of successful founders/owners choose in the more mature phase of their business's life cycle. In the previous chapter, we met recruitment business owner Rod Leefe. This is how he masterminded the further development of his business, Witan Jardine, over an eight-year period (Figure 5.1).

Between 2000 and 2008 the company was transformed from a generalist recruiter, filling accountancy positions at the more junior level, into a multi-function, multi-industry business partner, headhunting professionals for senior positions. If we take snapshots of the business in 2000 and 2008 and compare them, we see two very different companies bearing the same name. The transformation, however, did not take place overnight, but by a step-by-step process. We can track that development across a number of dimensions:

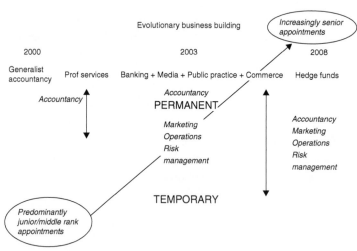

Figure 5.1 Evolutionary Business Building.
Source: Witan Jardine/Rod Leefe

- **By *client* profession/industry**: in 2000 Witan Jardine's primary market was an undifferentiated one, targeting its offer at anyone and everyone with a need for accountancy staff. The first move, following the BGP, was to focus on professional services firms, like the legal and insurance sectors, with comparable accounting needs. Within three years that client base had expanded to cover other service industries with similar needs, specifically banking, media, public practice [larger firms of accountants] and commerce [big commercial organisations]. Within five years the clientele now included the fast-growing sector of hedge funds.
- **By *candidate* profession**: in 2000 the candidate base was exclusively accountants. By 2003 that had grown to encompass Marketing, Operations and Risk Management.
- **By *type* of role**: in 2000 the roles filled were permanent ones. By 2003 the business was recruiting interim or temporary posts as well.
- **By *seniority* of role**: over that eight-year period Witan Jardine transitioned from "body-shopping" [as bulk recruitment is often described] to headhunting candidates for senior management positions.

This progression was hugely facilitated by the internal infrastructure Rod had put in place as a result of attending the BGP: the creation of the new role of client managers ["farmers"], whose remit was to nurture long-term relationships with key clients, as described previously. Clients that perceived Witan Jardine as a trusted partner, not merely as a commodity recruiting shop, were prepared to use their services more broadly. At some point a virtuous circle effect kicks in, as the list of reference sites ["who are your clients?"] becomes more impressive and builds the firm's credentials with new prospects. From the existing clients' point of view the perceived risk of using Witan Jardine also diminishes in proportion to the increase in their trust in the firm to deliver the right calibre of candidates. This in turn builds value in the business as it moves up the food chain from junior to senior roles, since the average net income in £ terms of each placement steadily grows.

The transformation of the company was unquestionably dramatic. As Figure 5.1 shows, a lot happened between 2000 and 2008. The pace of change was certainly rapid, yet controlled. Each foray into a new area was a stepping stone from the existing business into a new one. At no point was the core of the business in jeopardy, and at any point, if the expansion strategy stalled, it could be reined back in. At no point, indeed, did Rod "bet the farm".

REPEAT THE MAGIC FORMULA AND BET BIG

Another highly successful approach to managing the evolutionary strategy is to replicate a successful business recipe. In Chapter 3 we described how Moonpig founder Nick Jenkins doubled up repeatedly on his TV spend to attract new customers once he had proved the cost-effectiveness of this strategy – something he had learned from monitoring his competitors. Each campaign paid for itself within weeks, and the more he did, the bigger the impact on the success of the firm.

The "cloning" model follows a similar logic. We have already introduced the high-ropes outdoor adventure business, GoApe. When Tristram Mayhew took part in the Business Growth Programme in 2006, the company had five sites up and running. All were on land owned by England's Forestry Commission. In 2001 Tristram had concluded a deal with the Commission that allowed for developing six sites and granted exclusivity until 2006. As an incentive to GoApe to accelerate the roll-out, the Commission offered to extend the period of exclusivity to 26 years, if the Mayhews could open at least five venues within four years, which they duly did.

This push for more sites was part of the Forestry Commission's plan to diversify their income streams by creating visitor attractions. Up to that point the Commission's main source of revenue had been from logging and associated activities. The public were encouraged to visit the Commission's sites but did not do so in large numbers and did not spend money except in the few, rather basic cafés provided.

Not every site developed by GoApe up to 2005 was a commercial winner. Through trial and error, the Mayhews had learned that the surrounding demographics of a potential site and a relatively short driving time were the vital factors in determining its profitability. Choose the right location, close to a big enough, nearby population with high disposable incomes, and a site would pay for itself within eighteen to twenty-four months. Get it wrong and not only would payback take much longer, but the site would struggle to do much more than break even. Four of their existing sites were definitely in the right places but one was going to require considerable support to make a success of it.

The arrival of GoApe had also not gone unnoticed. During 2003 two British competitors opened similar style courses. One, Aerial eXtreme, was a joint venture backed by the biggest builder of poles-based high-ropes courses in the UK. The second, which was closest to GoApe in format[2] and only a few miles from GoApe's first site, was Extreeme [sic] Adventure, set up by a farmer seeking to diversify into the leisure sector.

By the end of 2004, GoApe was turning over £1.3 mn on its five sites and showing profits of around £170,000. The central dilemma that Tristram and Rebecca were wrestling with was this: in planning its expansion, should the business go deep or broad? *Going deep* meant exploiting additional revenue streams on the existing sites. There were three obvious opportunities, in the form of selling away-days to the corporate market, marketing add-ons such as clothing and related merchandise, and providing improved catering facilities. *Going broad* meant putting all the firm's efforts into locating and building new sites across the UK in areas not yet covered. Given the size of the business and its resources, it had to be one or the other.

FOOD FOR THOUGHT #13

By the autumn of 2005, Tristram and Rebecca Mayhew and their management team had resolved the question of expansion. Faced with a choice between consolidating their activities on the five existing GoApe sites and rolling out the business across the UK, the board had been unanimous that the company should focus on expansion. "Pre-empting the competition was a factor in our thinking," said Tristram. "But the clinching argument was creating career opportunities for our people. With just five sites they would have nowhere to go, and we would lose the talent in the business. We had always tried to offer terms and conditions at the top of the leisure industry, but the people we want are motivated by more than money."

The maximum rate of sustainable expansion was five, possibly six, new sites a year. The financing was in some respects the easiest issue to solve. With three years' trading behind him and a business model that worked, Tristram had managed to strike a deal with one of the more entrepreneurial of the British banks, Clydesdale. They were prepared to finance the business through an unsecured overdraft, lending effectively against future cashflows. For 2006 the plan was to open two new sites, making a total of seven. In May of that year, Tristram and fellow-director Will Galbraith attended the BGP. They started the programme thinking that they might aspire to have 15 or even 20 GoApe sites across Britain. By the end of the programme the other participants had convinced them that the target should be to have 40 sites by 2012!

Source: Go Ape case study

As it happens, by 2023 GoApe has managed to create just [!] 35 UK sites, ranging from Exeter to Aberdeen, and 14 in the United States. The cash generated from replicating the magic formula has allowed the business both to develop the pre-eminent national brand in its markets and to deepen the offer at its sites, providing low-ropes courses for younger children, for instance, and upgrading the catering facilities. The strategy has also provided the funds to design and build smaller urban GoApe formats in London at Alexandra Palace and Battersea Park.

BETTING *REALLY* BIG

As a closing thought on the topic of repeating the business recipe, but on a grand scale, we return to the story of serial entrepreneur Steve Jolliffe. In the last chapter we met Steve as the co-founder of Topgolf, a venture made possible by discovering how to fit a golf ball with a transmitting microchip capable of withstanding repeated shocks. Topgolf had reinvented the game of golf by turning the mundane driving range into an entertainment venue suitable for golfers and non-golfers alike. Apart from the novel technologies deployed, there were a number of ingredients necessary for the magic recipe to work:

- The game needed to be competitive, but so designed that non-golfers were not disadvantaged.
- The ancillary facilities – good hospitality, welcoming staff, adequate parking and so forth – had to be of a sufficiently high standard to justify a visit of at least two or three hours.
- The average spend per customer, generated partly by the hospitality offer, had to be enough to return a decent profit per venue.
- As well as a good initial visitor experience, continuous innovation was required, to ensure repeat trade and word-of-mouth marketing by loyal customers.

As Topgolf was developed around the world, however, it became clear to Steve that one of the concept's principal advantages was also a major downside. To develop a course required big money: the Las Vegas location on its own necessitated £70 mn of investment. This had the benefit of creating a barrier to entry by potential competitors. But it also meant long payback periods before investors were able to see a return on their money, which restricted the pool of potential partners.

The Jolliffe twins had secured, through patents, the technology behind Topgolf. Thinking about how they could use everything they had learned from this initial venture, they came up with the idea of reinventing mini-golf as their next business. In 2018 the first Puttshack was launched next to Bank station in the City of London. This time the venue is indoors and packaged as an evening's entertainment for groups of friends and work colleagues. It also relies on a similar mix of easy-going competition, novel course design, and hospitality, supported by the same technology. The advantage of this new concept is that the costs for each location are much lower and the return on investment is much quicker. Today there are 15 venues in the UK and the US in total, and the business is already valued at three-quarters of a billion dollars, supported by expansion capital of $150 mn supplied by Black Rock. According to Steve, next in line for a radical overhaul is the game of pool. And then he might think about retiring.

THE REVOLUTIONARY BUSINESS STRATEGY

When a business experiences a major shock, the only strategy for survival may well be that of radical reinvention. In the category of major shocks are:

- a major shift in technology, for example from analogue to digital
- the drying-up of a company's primary market
- dramatic changes in consumer preferences or behaviour
- drastic alterations in the supply chain

The best-known example of a business's failure to respond effectively to a major, indeed series, of market shocks, is probably the Kodak company [formally Eastman Kodak]. Until the late 1990s, it was the undisputed global leader in the photographic film industry. The first shock was in the form of the emergence of Japanese competitor Fujifilm, which took a huge share of the market. Then came the technology transition from film to digital technology. Even though Kodak actually developed the first self-contained digital camera, it was outcompeted by others. Multiple attempts to diversify from its core into digital photography and digital printing came to nothing and in January 2012 the company filed for Chapter 11 bankruptcy. It has since reformed and shed its legacy business, but its revenues are now a fraction of what they were, and the company is a specialist in industrial rather than consumer markets.

Kodak was a multi-billion-dollar corporation, and yet it could not withstand the turmoil in a market which the company believed that it owned. The impact of a dramatic market change on a typical owner/managed business with vastly smaller resources is likely to be overwhelming. The case of family business Ravensden provides a textbook illustration of how firms of this size can respond to sudden change, reinvent themselves from top to bottom, manage risk, and thrive.

FOOD FOR THOUGHT #14

Animal magic

When Mike Papé tells his story, he begins by describing the zoo of his childhood that existed in his back garden, and the exotic creatures such as penguins and sea lions that swam in pools. His teachers used to congratulate his parents on their child's powers of imagination. He might well have a vivid imagination, was their response, but the back garden was indeed full of pens and pools housing creatures from all over the world. Their home was a staging post for the animals that Ravensden's founders, Mike's parents Barry and Susan Papé, supplied to zoos, aquariums and safari parks in the UK and mainland Europe.

These days, if you've visited a well-known zoo, safari park or aquarium and bought a toy animal as a gift or souvenir, it's highly likely you have a Ravensden product in your home. And if you own a toy meerkat, you definitely have: to date Ravensden has supplied comparethemarket.com with over 300,000 Alexanders, Sergeis and the rest of the cast of characters. Look closely and you will see that they resemble their on-screen counterparts down to the tiniest detail.

The transition from live to toy animals was just the first in a series of transformational steps. The original business model had a limited future, once the company's customers had established their own breeding programmes, and so Barry and Susan invented a new revenue stream for their market from scratch. Their expertise in cross-border sourcing and import-export proved highly transferable, the major challenge being to identify a new supplier base. Other big developments include the company's first investment in a computer in 1982, a change to plc status, the ability to trade in multiple currencies, an online customer portal for 24/7 ordering and, most recently, a rebranding. This was more than just a new logo, but a complete review and overhaul of Ravensden's corporate identity. All communications media now feature the strapline "A world of animal companions", as a key element of its differentiation in a competitive marketplace. A big multinational might regard these changes as routine, but for a business that turns over a little more than £10 mn, each such step has a major impact.

Source: Ravensden plc

Like Witan Jardine, the "before and after" profiles of Ravensden are radically different. In each instance the businesses were transformed. But their evolutionary and revolutionary journeys were very different. Rod Leefe was able to develop his business progressively, step by step. The rapid changes at Ravensden's customer base of safari parks and zoos left the owners with little choice but to undertake a reinvention in short order, entailing a very different approach to managing the risks to the business. On the face of it, moving from dealing in live animals to selling toy ones looks fraught with hazard. In practice, Ravensden was able to capitalise on a number of inherent assets developed over the years:

- The customer base was largely the same. Zoos, aquariums and safari parks were well-established as visitor attractions in the UK by the 1980s. They might no longer have needed to buy live animals, but their shops required merchandise for visitors to take away as souvenirs.
- Ravensden had developed long-standing trading relationships with their customers, building trust and confidence.
- Within the business there was very considerable explicit and tacit knowledge of how to conduct cross-border trading, both import and export.
- Ravensden's history had given the company an excellent understanding of the shape and appearance of live animals. The detailed briefings given to manufacturers resulted in life-like toys. In Mike's opinion, it is the company's biggest competitive advantage: "we know what animals look like!" Today the range runs to around 1400 product lines, with 200–250 additions annually, and in a post-Brexit world, the company does just under 38% of its turnover with the EU.

The biggest unknown and potential risk was finding suitable manufacturers, and the company was greatly assisted by the rise and growing sophistication of factories in the Far East. Converting to plc[3] status also assisted in reducing any perceived risk on the part of buyers.

With the company's first fifty years behind it, the second generation is assuming an increasing role in the business. For the moment, the lesson from the Ravensden case is that the risks of radical reinvention can be managed effectively through identifying and transferring the accrued assets that have served a business well into the next stage of its evolution.

THINKING OF SELLING? FIRST MAKE YOURSELF REDUNDANT ...

When Lara Morgan sold the majority of her shares in Pacific Direct in 2008, she was already living nearly 100 miles away from the company's head office in Bedford. She and her family had relocated to the Wiltshire countryside and were refurbishing an old property. A new chief executive was running the daily operations of the business, responsible for making all decisions that did not require board approval. Lara visited the company roughly once a month in her capacity as Chairman. "I knew that I was going to sell Pacific," she said. "I wanted to show that the business was perfectly capable of running without me, so that I wouldn't be tied in to the deal after the sale went through."

As a critical step in advance of sale, Lara had changed her role in the organisation. Unlike Adam Nemenyi, who saw a continuing future at Aerospares 2000, Lara had concluded that her time at Pacific was coming to an end. As well as crystallising the value that she had created, she had plans to embark on a new chapter in her life.

FOOD FOR THOUGHT #15

Stepping up: The transition from CEO to Chairman. Extracted from the author's blog

I recently spent an afternoon with some of the most successful entrepreneurs I know. Between them they have founded or bought into a diverse set of businesses, covering training, financial services, luxury cosmetics, market research, telecomms management, media services and executive recruitment. Most were in their forties and operating in the UK.

In the two decades that I have been running businesses, advising entrepreneurs and serving on company boards, I have constantly returned to this central question: how does a venture founder create a business with independent value? Most owner-managed firms don't wean themselves off their dependency on their founders. The consequence is that the option of selling – certainly for the kind of price the owner(s) may want for the business – is never really on the table. I was staggered to read the other day that only 7% of attempts to sell private UK businesses are successful. The other 93% apparently just soldier on, and eventually either cease to trade or change ownership for a nominal amount.

There are many reasons why business sales fall through. But experience and intuition suggest to me that the major factor why most attempted sales never get off the starting block is that there is nothing of any real value to a prospective buyer. A large part of that value arises out of creating a business that runs independently of the founder. To achieve this, the founder has to learn to let go …. For many entrepreneurs a significant milestone in that journey is reached when they cease to be the CEO or MD and step up to the role of Chairman★ of their own business.

How do you know it's time to let go?

To return to our round-table discussion, one of the first questions to surface was knowing when the time was ripe to hand over the operational reins to a successor. One participant, Chairman of a multi-million-pound financial services group, spoke of a dawning awareness that the business which he had laboured night and day to set up was re-cast in his mind *as an asset*: to be sure, a very important asset, but in a sense no different from his stock portfolio or pension fund. Once he had crossed that bridge mentally, it was a no-brainer. Promote and recruit the best managerial talent he could find – invariably better at specific tasks than he was – and then create the conditions in which they could thrive. In other words, maximise the performance of the asset, not pander to his own whims and ego.

Others shared his view. And, as more self-revelation was put on the table, the word *boredom* cropped up. Being CEO of your own business is, after all, a job. Other people get bored if they're in a job too long. Boredom is almost certainly a sign that, on a day-to-day basis, the business can get along quite nicely without you. It's actually a positive signal, but it's potentially quite destructive. I've known too many entrepreneurs who suffer from a low boredom threshold. Without meaning to, they react to feeling bored by meddling and interfering for the sake of it, demoralising their staff and often causing many more problems than they solve. That's because they're confronting what ought to be another symptom that the business is ready for the change: *the founder no longer understands [some of] the details of how the business works.* For many entrepreneurs that's a reason to panic. Others embrace it. As another participant in the discussion put it: "I knew we were ready for me to change roles when someone produced a brilliant set of measurement indicators at a meeting. I hadn't asked for them, they'd just gone ahead and done it. Much better than anything I'd come up with. I asked when we were going to implement them. I was told we'd been using them for three months. Time for me to get kicked upstairs!"

Appointing your successor

The dream scenario is to have an obvious internal candidate for the MD's job, a seamless handover, and everyone lives happily ever after. For most people, however, that scenario is just a dream. Our executive recruiter gave some robust and practical advice. First and foremost it's a job, he pointed out. What's more, it's an important job and a big investment: when you factor in all the costs involved in the search and selection process, salary and benefits for at least two years, it could be north of £250,000 even for quite a modest business. If you were spending that much on a piece of machinery, you'd invest some thought and care in the decision. He also pointed out that all the research showed most people were pretty poor at recruitment. It ought to be a scientific process, undertaken by experts in the field (note: since he has recently sold his business, he has no vested interest in pushing this line!).

There was general agreement that, even if an ideal internal candidate existed, he or she should be measured against a full job spec., drawn up independently. That spec. may well look like the opposite of the founder. If he or she is a typical entrepreneur, with a flair for invention, solving problems and – in the nicest sense – self-promotion, the chances are you need someone with a head for detail, systems and processes who enjoys the steady-state challenges of managing operations. And if you are recruiting someone from a corporate background, with a view to bringing with them the disciplines of a professional manager, make sure they fully understand what it's like to work in a smaller, entrepreneurial business. For at least half the people around the table that was the crunch issue, based on personal experience of recruiting corporate types who couldn't hack an environment lacking in big company infrastructure.

Managing the transition

It's good for a business to be shaken up from time to time was the general view. By all means prepare the ground, but don't pussyfoot around. Everyone needs to get the message that there's a new sheriff in town. One of our participants moved out of his office and just keeps a desk in the corner, to lower his profile in the business. He comes into the company from time to time, but deliberately holds meetings with his CEO off-site, to avoid any hint of undermining his successor. Harking back to the theme of regarding the business as an asset, everyone recommended that the new Chairman have plenty of outside interests and, if these were lacking, develop them fast. One contributor who couldn't make it on the day wrote saying that for the six months following the appointment he busied himself with other things. Be prepared to bite your lip, he advised. The new CEO will deliver what you consider to be 50% of what you did, which your successor rates at 150%. You'll be told that the systems you installed are woefully inadequate and some of your longest-serving, loyal staff are not up to their jobs. You might not like what you hear, but the new man or woman must have the opportunity to build their own team around them.

On the other hand, be absolutely clear about your vision for the business and the paramount task of the CEO, which is to deliver it. As Chairman I have really only one job, said my correspondent: to fire the CEO if he fails to deliver!

So what should the Chairman *ACTUALLY DO*?

Well, there was plenty of discussion around this one. The fact is, no two Chairmen's jobs look exactly the same. An important distinction that emerged is the difference between businesses with and without external shareholders. If the business has institutional or private investors, then there's a good chance that the primary role of the Chairman will be to manage the board and shareholders. Another contributor who couldn't make it on the day has a business with over twenty outside investors. He has been part-time chairman of the business for about a year now, and nearly all of that time is taken up in board business and conversations with shareholders – mostly on the subject of when and how the business will be sold.

The same contributor made another point. Entrepreneurs shouldn't confuse being bored with the role of CEO with being bored with the business. Those who do, risk selling their businesses prematurely and regretting it. Since he changed roles to become Chairman his enthusiasm for the business had been reinvigorated. He also sees it with fresh eyes and can offer his successor a more detached perspective.

For those who don't spend most of their time as Chairman managing their board and shareholders, there's a variety of opinion as to what the job should consist of. Strategy, finance, recruitment and new business development were all mentioned. The reality, however, seems to be that it's horses for courses, a mix of the skills and talents of the entrepreneur and the needs of the business. On three points there was general consensus:

First, becoming Chairman creates the time and space to think strategically about the business, so it makes good sense to take that opportunity. This does not mean the Chairman should have exclusive ownership of formulating and reviewing strategy. Indeed, the bigger the business, the more the need to involve others in the process. But it would be an exceptional situation for an owner-manager to relinquish a leading role in creating the strategy for the business they have built over the years.

Second, like it or not, the entrepreneur will continue to be viewed as the figurehead and ambassador for the business by staff, customers, suppliers and other key stakeholders. That's just a fact of business life.

Third, this is the ideal time to review the composition of the board, indeed the whole business of corporate governance. If you have external shareholders and non-execs already, you will do this as a matter of course. If not, you will need to consider whether you have the right skills and experience on the board to support the new CEO in his or her role, and to take the business forward to the next stage. One contributor told how he had conducted a careful search to recruit a non-exec. who would function as mentor to the new MD, and who could also as an intermediary between two people he described as chalk and cheese.

How do you know if you're doing a good job (as Chairman)?

If you have outside shareholders and a robust board to report to, they'll soon let you know! But most people in this situation are likely to be majority shareholders and the dominant figures in the business. So how should you assess your own accountability? Avoid the temptation to invent new or unnecessary performance indicators was the general view. The external reporting measures are the ones that count. Is the business delivering its targets? Is it on track to achieve the shared vision of the Chairman, the board and the CEO? If it is, then you're doing a good job. If not, it's time to sit down and take stock. Often the hardest thing for many owner-managers to take on board is an acceptance that they will contribute more by doing less.

Some dos and don'ts

Do

> Consider whether this is right for you, the staff and the business. If the answer is yes to all three, you've passed the test
>
> Develop outside interests if you don't already have them
>
> Prepare the business, but don't fudge the decision once you've made it
>
> Give your successor time and space to breathe
>
> Be ready to take on responsibility for development of the board
>
> Remember that becoming chairman may mean giving up things you enjoy doing

Don't

> Get in the way of the new regime
>
> Take inevitable changes personally: it really is just business.
>
> And finally... remember that in times of crisis, the role of the Chairman will come into its own.

*Chairman is used in a gender-neutral way, in conformance with the general usage of the term.

©David Molian 2023

PREPARING FOR SALE

By no means everyone who decides to sell their business will go through this process of transition from an executive to a non-executive role. It does, though, have three big advantages:

- It puts clear blue water between the owner/manager and the business, making a clean break easier to argue for if that's what the seller wants
- It accustoms the people in the business to a change of management style and, quite possibly, practice
- It forces the owner/manager to develop interests outside the business

Regardless of whether this route appeals, there are a number of other elements to preparing for sale which are key to making the process a smoother ride.

GETTING TO THE MAGIC NUMBER

We referred to this before, in the story of Adam Nemenyi's sale of Aerospares 2000. It's the sum which you are prepared to sell the business for, and very rarely is it plucked randomly out of the air. Rather it's the culmination of:

- Some hard thinking about what financial independence would look like for yourself and your dependents. What do you actually need?
- Assessing what the business might realistically be valued at, if presented in the most attractive light.

At some point you will need to seek expert advice to see whether these two figures match, or whether there is further work required to get the valuation of the business to reach the magic number. Although each situation is unique, based on our observations over many years there are some general principles that are important to bear in mind:

- A strong recent track record of turnover and profit growth is not an infallible guide to future potential, but it does build confidence in the minds of potential acquirers.
- A business model built on recurrent, predictable future revenues is valued more highly than a business that depends on a constant search for short-term sources of income. Basically, long-term contracts are gold-dust.
- It might seem like stating the obvious, but a business is valued differently by various potential buyers who each have different reasons for buying. Adam Nemenyi's buyer was a private equity consolidator looking to "buy and build", with a view to selling eventually an entity whose sum was greater than its constituent parts. The business may have been less valuable to a trade buyer. The job of a corporate finance professional is to broaden the field of potential acquirers to achieve the right deal for their client.
- When an acquiring company looks at a potential purchase of a privately-held business, it commonly looks at "comparables" – that's to say recent transactions in the same sector which set a benchmark for valuation. The more you and your corporate finance advisors are able to argue that your business is better or different from such comparables, the greater the chances of commanding a price premium.
- The magic number provides a focal point in negotiations.

It is also worth adding that having a clear and settled view about the magic number is less likely to produce "seller's remorse".

KNOWING WHAT YOU'RE GOING TO, AS WELL AS GOING FROM

The average person across the world born in 1960, the earliest year the United Nations began collating global data, could expect to live to 52.5 years of age. For those born today, that same figure is over 70. In the UK specifically, it is currently around 80 years for men and 84 years for women. If you sell a business in your forties or fifties, you have in all likelihood decades to look forward to. What do you want to do with the rest of your life? It's possible that you might want to spend five days a week on the golf course or a boat, but most people – like Alex Fagioli in Chapter Three – find the novelty soon wears off. Besides this, most of your social network are still busy at work during office hours. When we look at BGP participants who have sold their businesses while still physically active, the majority are pursuing a portfolio life as investors, advisors, mentors, philanthropists and non-executive directors of other businesses. Some are pursuing long-held dreams which financial independence makes possible, such as owning a boutique hotel or spending time on sports photography. The happiest seem to be those who have a purposeful plan – and they are also least likely to suffer seller's remorse.

PREPARE TO MODIFY YOUR BEHAVIOUR[4]

Imagine that you, the founder and owner of a successful private company, are sitting across the table from a potential trade buyer and their advisors. It's the most likely scenario for the sale of a privately held business. You are proud of what you have achieved, and rightly so. For years you have been in the habit of promoting the qualities and capabilities of your firm to customers, suppliers, staff and probably anyone else who's prepared to listen: after all, it's a great company.

If the trade buyer is a significant organisation, their representative is very probably a salaried employee. He or she may well be comfortably off, but they're never going to enjoy the kind of big payday coming your way if a deal is agreed. Instead they will be working for the next however many years until they can afford to retire. They are fully aware that the purchase of your business is going to make you [comparatively] rich. It would be superhuman not to experience at least a little resentment. There's some bridge-building required on your part, and it's called *giving the buyer permission to buy.*

Instead of extolling your achievements, as even the most modest founder falls into the habit of doing, you acknowledge your limitations. You have taken the business as far as you can. To secure its future, and exploit its full potential, the business needs the kind of professional expertise a company such as x can bring as the new owner. Humility is the order of the day, and it may make the difference between a good sale and a great one.

SELLING A BUSINESS IS A FULL-TIME JOB

Once the clock has started ticking, the process of selling is likely to be all-consuming. As owner you are one of a handful of key individuals [discussed below] who are integral to making the deal happen. That is why it is essential to have a senior team in place capable of running the day-to-day operations of the business and makes another strong argument for your having made yourself more or less redundant. The experiences of BGP participants suggest that the process of selling a business can take up to two years from start to finish, and even then, there is no guarantee that a deal will not fall through at some stage.

TIE UP ANY LOOSE ENDS AT THE OUTSET

If a potential acquirer is serious, a process of due diligence will kick in, when their advisors will look to comb through every piece of information and document that has a bearing on the value of your business. Among the critical ones are shareholders' agreements and articles of association, contracts of employment, the register of assets, current agreements with customers and suppliers, and evidence of compliance with all statutory legislation governing your industry. Any corporate finance advisor should provide a comprehensive list. The critical point is that missing or incomplete information is a chink in your armour and a potential risk the purchaser can cite as a reason for reducing the offer price. Lara Morgan, for example, created a virtual "document room", in which anything that might have a bearing on the sale of her business was stored electronically [see also below].

FINALLY, "QUALITY" OF EARNINGS

This is an expression widely used by specialists in corporate transactions. If you're unfamiliar with it, the phrase may seem strange. A pound is a pound is a pound, after all. In the world of acquisition, however, not all pounds are created equal. The most widely used method of valuation begins with establishing your firm's EBITDA, that is Earnings [trading profit] Before Interest, Tax, Depreciation and Amortisation [of intellectual property and goodwill write-offs arising from any prior acquisitions]. Without getting too technical, it is fair to say that this serves as a handy proxy for your business's ability to generate cash from its trading activity. That figure is then multiplied by a number – "the multiple", for example 3, 5, or 7, to arrive at a price. The higher the multiple, the greater the valuation.

It is in the choice of the multiple that "quality" of earnings comes into play. In any individual market sector there is an average or typical multiple, which is derived partly from looking at how public companies are valued on stock markets. Construction companies, for example, tend to be accorded relatively low multiples compared with technology stocks. References at the end of this chapter provide suggestions for exploring why this is the case. For present purposes, it is enough to say that a seasoned corporate transaction adviser will guide you on the best way to raise that multiple, and thus the quality of earnings, from the time at which you decide to sell: all the more reason to begin such conversations sooner rather than later.

THE KEY PEOPLE INVOLVED IN THE SALE

In the normal course of events, on your side of the table are three vital individuals: you as the owner, your finance director and your corporate adviser.

- **Your role** is to provide clarity over what you want [and are prepared to concede], taking account not only of more narrow concerns such as your magic number but other issues such as the continuing health of the company and its workforce.
- **Your finance director's role** is to be on top of all the financial and contractual data which bear on the value of the business.
- **Your corporate adviser** is there to steer you through the process, stay several steps ahead regarding potential obstacles, advise on what is worth fighting over and what is not, and deflect some of the heat that often arises when negotiations become intense.

This trio is pretty much a constant presence throughout the deal. Called in as required will be your accountants [who may also act as your corporate advisers], whose role is to verify and validate claims made about the firm; and the lawyers who will prepare the contracts relating to the sale.

Most people will only ever sell a business once. The benefit of doing something for the second or third time is the opportunity to learn from your own experience. If you only have one shot, you rely heavily on the experience of others. At this point, the time spent earlier in the life of your company on upgrading your professional advisers and building your personal networks comes into its own. Mine your contact base. There is a bewildering multitude of people out there who will gladly take your money. Take your time over choosing a corporate adviser who meets all your requirements and, ideally, comes highly recommended from someone who can vouch for their professionalism.

ACCELERANTS

Prepare your "data room" well in advance: The data room is the virtual storage system you create for filing all information – as listed above – which relates to the due diligence process.

Many BGPers who have concluded successful sales believe that doing this well in advance was fundamental to concluding a timely deal at their desired price.

Unearth any skeletons in the cupboard and address them: A major benefit of assembling the data room early on is discovering anything that might detract from the deal during the due diligence process. This could include significant sales or procurement contracts that are due to expire or are loosely worded, documents that are missing, contracts of employment that no longer comply with legislation, environmental or supply chain audits that are overdue, non-compliance with health and safety legislation, and so forth. Adam Nemenyi recommends doing this every few years in any case, as a form of company MOT test.

BEARTRAPS AND BLOCKERS

Ensure the personal chemistry is right: During the process of selling, it is likely you will spend more time with your advisory team than anyone else in your life. It will be intense and pressured. Be sure that, at the very least, you do not actively dislike the people you work with.

Telling the right [internal] people at the right time: It is up to you how open or closed you choose to be about disclosing what is happening during the sales process. As a private company you are not constrained by the requirements of public markets [though your acquirer may be]. Even if you have strong instincts about who you tell and at what stage, it is better to agree upfront on a schedule of communications with your adviser, rather than regret a rash disclosure that leads to problems.

AND FINALLY: ALTERNATIVE APPROACHES TO REALISING VALUE

A final trade sale might be the commonest form of realising value for the business founder/owner, but it is not the only option. In the case of Steve Jolliffe's ventures, Topgolf and latterly Puttshack, the sale of part of the founders' equity at various points as new partners have invested has released some of that value along the way. Nick Jenkins also attracted multiple rounds of investors, both private and institutional, to support the growth of Moonpig, but their money as well as his own reinvestment stayed in the business until the eventual sale to Photobox in 2011.[5] To realise their ambitious plans for Hotel Chocolat, Angus Thirlwell and co-founder Peter Harris listed the business on AIM, the junior market of the London Stock Exchange on 5th May 2016. Within five days the value of the business had jumped by 28%. According to the *Guardian*, the placement raised £55 mn, of which £43 mn went to the founders and the rest to fund new shops, improve its website and increase production capacity. The two-thirds stake retained by Angus and Peter was valued on the 10th May at £140 mn. The amount of news coverage reflected not just the fame of the brand, but the rarity of such events for owner-managed businesses.

If the paramount consideration is the future wellbeing of employees and the preservation of a distinctive company culture, the transfer of ownership into an Employee Ownership Trust [EOT] is an attractive option. Since 2012 the UK government has promoted this scheme as the main route to giving employees a long-term stake in their company's future. It also has tax advantages for the seller. In 2019 the board of GoApe had instructed advisers to seek buyers for the business. As Tristram and Rebecca told the *Financial Times* in August 2022, now the couple were entering their sixth decade they felt they no longer lived up to their own strapline of living life adventurously. They hankered after a life beyond GoApe, and they wanted to explore it. However, the process of finding a buyer proved more challenging than expected and the Covid-19 outbreak did not help: 90% of the staff were placed on furlough and all the company's sites were closed. Turnover fell and the business limped along on government support.

During this period the continuing commitment and loyalty of their workforce made the couple re-think their priorities. They returned to the idea of a sale to their employees, which they had previously rejected on being told that it would raise less money than a trade sale. After discussion with other shareholders in 2021, it was agreed that 90% of the shares would be sold to an Employee Ownership Trust, with the Mayhews retaining 10%. The deal is structured so that payment for the shares takes place over a number of years, and the composition of the EOT board is split 50/50 between employees and founders. GoApe is not the only BGP business to go down this path: in 2021 secondary glazing specialists Selectaglaze did the same thing when Chairman Meredith Childerstone [BGP 2000] transferred the family business into an EOT. The scheme is still in its infancy: according to the FT, there are only 800 employee-owned businesses in the UK, but the movement is growing. Two hundred and fifty have been created since March 2020 and well-known names include organic farmbox delivery service Riverford and home entertainment specialist Richer Sounds.

SUMMARY

- If the founder/owner believes that their business has unexploited potential, they need to ask themselves two fundamental questions: is the business capable of scale; and am I the person capable of the necessary change to take it on that journey? If the answer to both is yes, then you can commit to the long haul.
- If the business has invented and proved a "magic formula" that can be replicated and scaled, this is a great way to pursue further growth by "betting big".
- This more mature phase of the journey also carries with it risks: the founder/owner can mitigate these risks by consciously deciding whether the next phase of growth is *evolutionary* or *revolutionary*. Either way, the business that results will look very different from what it was like before.

- The evolutionary route manages risk by transforming a business progressively, step by step, so that the core of the firm's activities is never put in jeopardy.
- The revolutionary route is a response to factors which threaten the existing business model, making it no longer viable, and provides an alternative path that ensures not just survival but the means of capturing new opportunities for growth. Revolutionary reinvention manages and mitigates risk by capitalising on existing assets that are transferrable into the new business model.
- The successful sale of a business rests as much on careful preparation as negotiation in the room. Critical to success are:

  - a tight-knit team of three [the owner, the Finance Director and the Corporate Advisor] working on the deal
  - a watertight data room that covers all potential liabilities
  - a competent CEO taking care of the day-to-day business

- Clarity over the next phase of your life minimises seller's regret.
- Alternative ways of realising value – apart from a trade sale – may better meet your needs and values.

NOTES

1 "There are known knowns. These are things we know that we know. There are known unknowns. That is to say, there are things that we know we don't know" (February 12th, 2002).
2 It even adopted the same colour scheme for branding purposes.
3 plc stands for public limited company, although the shares in the case of Ravensden are still wholly owned by the Papé family. The costs of reporting compliance are higher, but many larger customers prefer to trade with a plc rather than with a limited company.
4 For this insight I am grateful to Brian Livingston, Managing Director, Oaklins Evelyn Partners, formerly partner of Smith & Williamson.

5 After sale, a business's future can take many twists and turns. Photobox was subsequently acquired by private equity capital in 2015, and the Moonpig Group, comprising the UK and Dutch businesses, is now listed separately on the London Stock Exchange. At March 2023 it was valued at roughly ten times the amount when sold in 2011. It often pays the founder/owner to retain a vestigial shareholding from the original sale!

FURTHER READING

For a good discussion of creating value which outperforms sector multiples, see John Rosling's *The Secrets of the Seven Alchemists*, already referred to.

On the process of business exits, see Guy Rigby's *From Vision to Exit: The Entrepreneur's Guide to Building and Selling a Business*, Harriman House

On the preparation for business exit, see www.coutts.com/content/dam/rbs-coutts/coutts-com/Files/entrepreneurs-reports/Long_Goodbye.pdf

For an enlightening discussion of the variation of valuation multiples across different industries, see the discussion on Quora, www.quora.com/Why-do-multiples-vary-so-much-by-industry

On creating an Employee Ownership Trust, see www.gov.uk/employee-ownership. The advantages are set out on the PWC website at www.pwc.co.uk/services/tax/employee-ownership-trusts.html#:~:text=Employee%20Ownership%20Trusts%20(EOTs)%20are,free%20from%20capital%20gains%20tax.

Many corporate broking firms provide free seminars that explain the selling process. Take advantage!

AFTERWORD

Jamie Waller [BGP 2010] founded the JBW Group in 2004 and sold the business twelve years later in 2016, while still in his late thirties. Today he is a philanthropist, ambassador for the Prince's Trust, active investor, published author, and still somehow finds time to run an early-stage business. In conversation with the author in mid-2023, he talks about what triggered the sale of his first business, and what happened next.

The Author: Could you give us a brief description of the JBW Group at the time you first decided to sell? What were its activities, how many people did you employ, where were your locations, and what was the financial profile?

JW: JBW Group was an outsourcing company focused on UK government debt analytics and recovery. We were around 170 people across two UK locations and had a PBT [profit before tax] of approximately £3 m.

DOI: 10.4324/9781003410614-7

The Author: How did you know it was time to sell JBW Group? Was there a trigger?

JW: JBW was always for sale. The philosophy was: build a business, make some money, bank it and de-risk my life. The selling target, however, kept changing: first £10 m, then an offer would be made, so £20 m, another offer would be made, and then finally we committed to the process, appointed advisors, and put the business up for sale. We then sold for over £40 m.

The Author: When you made the decision to sell, did you have a clear vision of what you wanted to do next?

JW: Yes, JBW was known as an outsourcing firm but the reality was that we were a tech business. Our tech enabled us to deliver industry-leading margins and a superior service. The reality however was that we were not going to make technology multiples on a sale, so I divested the technology into a different business and licensed it back to JBW post-sale. Six days after selling JBW I launched Hito, a FinTech business in the debt management industry. We launched with JBW as our first customer.

The Author: What – if any – was your priority list of things to do after the sale of JBW Group?

JW: Hito was the priority, and we built that business up over nine months and were offered over £9 m for its sale – we took it. Making £1 m a month was difficult to turn down. Looking back, I think I should have given myself more of a break after selling JBW. Post Hito, however, was different. Sudden unemployment came as a shock! I felt a little lost, and made a decision to focus on my family.

Almost everyone on their deathbed regrets not spending more time with their children when they were young. So I bought a yacht and decided to sail with them halfway around the world. My children were babies, so from 2017–2022 we sailed 7500 miles around the Med. I also set up an investment fund, invested in 13 different companies, purchased one outright and started another tech business in the debt management space. It was a fun five years.

The Author: What has surprised you most about the next phase of your life?

JW: Not having one single purpose. When you are growing a business, you are all in, 100% focused on one north star. I found the absence of that very difficult. A friend once said to me: never sell your business and become "rich and irrelevant". Don't become the guy at the networking events telling people what you once did. No one will care. He was right.

I worked with a coach in 2018 to re-ignite my passion for the industry I had been part of for so many years and in 2019 started my third business, Just. This has been an amazing journey and I am loving start-up days again. I also started a department for the Prince's Trust called the Enterprise Network and I served as Chair during that period also. It was an absolute privilege to serve the Prince of Wales and for the later part of my time there, the King. From 2019–2023 I started and built the Prince's Trust Enterprise Network from an idea into a nationwide network of entrepreneurs who have donated nearly £2 m.

The Author:	And what has given you most pleasure in the next phase of your life?
JW:	Time with my family and time on the sea. I love the ocean and am now planning to sail around the world in 2025, home school the children and spend more time building the most amazing memories.
The Author:	Do you plan your time in detail or do you leave space for the unexpected?
JW:	I am terrible at this! I work whenever I am awake and take on far too much, but I love what I do. However, every three months I organise a day with my PA to review how I spent the last three months, and see if I can use my time more effectively. It never works.
The Author:	What is the single most important thing in your life now? And is that different from when you were running the JBW Group?
JW:	Difficult to answer this, but honestly, it's my health and wellbeing. If I am fit, healthy and strong I can continue to help thousands in my philanthropy, I can continue to start, grow and sell businesses, and I can be the best husband and dad to my family. All of these things are important to me.
The Author:	What three pieces of advice would you give to a business founder who is thinking of exiting their business?
JW:	First, think about you, not just the business and the price. At the same time as you appoint an advisor, appoint for yourself a coach to develop a plan for your "life after exit". Second, appoint an advisor you can work with, not one who sells to you the best. It can be a bumpy ride, so do it with someone you can trust. Third, take some time off

after selling and before jumping into anything again – a minimum of six months.

The Author: Anything else to add?

JW: It's emotional, it's difficult, and a life without purpose is a life that is miserable. Learn from me and tens of my friends who have made the same mistakes and please, please, please, plan, plan, plan. I was lucky, I kept re-iterating my "life after exit" as I went along and had ample opportunities present themselves to me. Others might not be so fortunate and find themselves "rich and irrelevant".